NCL

D0581090

TE...
R...
TO ADOLESCENTS

PIERRE BABIN, o.m.i.

J. P. BAGOT

LONDON
BURNS & OATES

BURNS & OATES LIMITED
25 Ashley Place, London, S.W.1

First publication in Great Britain, 1968

Teaching Religion to Adolescents is a translation and adaptation of two works by Père Pierre Babin, O.M.I., and Abbé J. P. Bagot: *Dix Conseils pour la causerie de Catéchèse à des adolescents* and *Orientations pédagogiques pour une Catéchèse de préadolescents de milieu scolaire*, originally published in the *Le Sel de la Terre* series by Maison Mame, Paris, copyright 1962.

This translation was done at Marianopolis College, Montreal, by Religious of the Congregation de Notre Dame, and the adaptation was made by the Reverend William B. Thompson, O.M.I., Catholic Central High School, London, Ontario.

NIHIL OBSTAT

John A. Fournier, C.S.B.
February 27, 1967

IMPRIMATUR

✠ Lawrence P. Whelan
Auxiliary Bishop of Montreal
March 7, 1967

S.B.N.: 223 97649 0

Reproduced and printed in Great Britain by
Fletcher & Son Ltd, Norwich

Contents

Foreword

Those engaged in religious instruction of adolescent boys and girls will find in these pages many penetrating insights into the problem of the presentation of the mystery of salvation to young people.

The conscientious teacher should not expect from this book the mechanics of a drill book but rather numerous counsels and suggestions on which he may draw freely to prepare himself for the transmission of God's Word to his young hearers.

The teachers' guidelines for the catechesis of adolescents herein presented were developed by several research teams working under the guidance and the inspiration of Father Pierre Babin, O.M.I. Participating institutes and groups are Le Centre de Recherche de Pédagogie Religieuse de l'Adolescence; students of the Institut Supérieur Catéchétique Paris; and students of the Licence d'Enseignement Religieux, Lyon.

These guidelines refer often to the conclusions of an inquiry made among 2,000 adolescents of varying ages and backgrounds. The question asked of these adolescents is, "What are your ideas about a well-run religious class?" Their replies provided the data upon which the conclusions of the inquiry are based. Certain conclusions of special interest were drawn from the work of Sister Madeleine-Thérèse and Sister Marguerite-Marie, students at the Institut Supérieur Catéchétique of Paris.

Quotations not otherwise identified within the text are taken from answers given by adolescents to the research question. Specific reference to the sources of some answers are given only when it is useful to distinguish remarks made by boys and girls or by pupils in particular age groups.

The guidelines drawn from the research have been verified and published by Father Pierre Babin and Abbé J. P. Bagot, members of the Sous-Commission du Centre National de l'Enseignement Religieux. They are not directives. They are the outcome of a special inquiry and aim only to provide notes useful for catechists and other educators in their work.

Centre de Recherche de Pédagogie Religieuse de l'Adolescence
    Paris: Centre National, 19, rue de Varenne
    Lyon: Direction de l'Enseignment Religieux,
        6, avenue Adolphe-Max

Ten Counsels for the Catechesis of Adolescents

I. The catechist is spiritually attentive to the adolescent.

II. The catechist is himself.

III. The catechist organizes the development of the catechesis so that the whole personality of the student is involved.

IV. The catechist conducts discussion according to effective technique so indispensable in the formation of a free and responsible person.

V. The catechist develops discussion so as to stimulate active progress in understanding and in faith.

VI. The catechist enlivens discussion by recalling personal experiences and current events.

VII. The catechist provides formal structure for his catechesis.

VIII. The catechist makes the lesson itself an aid to memorization.

IX. The catechist varies the form of discussion.

X. The catechist varies the method for class prayers.

PART ONE · *The Catechist*

I. Ten Counsels for the Catechist Teaching Adolescents

The personal attitude of the catechist has a bearing on the message which he has the mission to transmit.

I. The catechist is spiritually attentive to the adolescent.

The catechesis of adolescents is conditioned by the bond of sympathy between the catechist and his students, sympathy governed by human norms and rooted in true Christian love.

The catechist gives special consideration to the following points:

He relaxes and calms his mind before going into class. The ideal catechist is not a bustling teacher, lost in his specialty.

He looks at his students through the eyes of Christ. He banishes all irrelevant preoccupations. He surrenders himself to the action of Christ, to His way of seeing and of loving. He has faith in the young and in the power of grace. The more he believes in his students, the better he will make them ready to receive Christ.

He is not obsessed with what he is going to say; rather he is docile to the Holy Spirit. He adopts a spiritual attitude toward persons, human details, concrete facts. Many classroom situations, for example, may arise affecting conditions under which a particular lesson is taught. The catechist is not upset by such contingencies as electrical failure in the building, sickness of students, tension created by examination jitters, or daydreaming that characterizes spring fever. He might make such concrete situations the starting point for the religion class, much as St. Paul in Athens began his catechesis by referring to the statue "To the Unknown God." (Acts 17:22ff.)

II. The catechist is himself.

Adolescents do not like those who play roles, who ply their trade self-consciously. Spontaneously, they ask sincerity and truth;

they like the direct, genuine teacher. The catechist accepts his own personality with its impulsiveness, sometimes even its whims and fancies. But it is himself he accepts just as he is. The important thing is to live in the truth of Christ, to be and to appear, not a perfect person, but a truly sincere and genuine person in the presence of the Word.

He does not neglect his own unique charisma under the pretext that he is submerging himself for the sake of a well-thought-out pedagogy adapted to adolescence. Undoubtedly some types of teachers are attuned to the mentality of young people. They are most themselves, so to speak, when they are with their students. But those who are less at ease, less at home with the adolescent, who are inclined to a more intellectual approach to things, who are deductive and rational by nature, should not be led to discount the potentialities inherent in their temperament. These qualities— intellectual and rational—are genuinely human and personal. Teachers so inclined can certainly "come across" in the catechetical situation. More than others, however, they will be careful to prepare lively, concrete discussions with plenty of examples, realizing that a too intellectual or abstract approach is not ordinarily attractive to adolescents. Nevertheless, they should not be afraid to be themselves. Their students will respect and love them for it.

On the emotional plane, the catechist is not continually trying to repress himself. If the day's weather makes him more dynamic, so much the better. If not, there are so many helps which can be used to good advantage as attractive, relaxing ways and means for him to convey his message. This is where such things as records, movies, slides, or easy dialogue with the young people suit the occasion.

While the catechist should not be a "weather man", the dynamism of whose teaching fluctuates with the barometer, nevertheless it is good for adolescents to realize that grace has not destroyed nature in the teacher, and that he enjoys in the Lord a deep and broad freedom embracing all that is human. He teaches in real, concrete human situations and presents himself accordingly. He has his good days, as the students have, and those which are not so good. Personal problems, distractions of one kind or another, the nameless feeling of being less sharp at times than he would like to be, are all human conditions that variously affect his teaching. The catechist learns to handle them in the best way, for himself and for the adolescents he is teaching.

III. The catechist organizes the development of the catechesis so that the whole personality of the student is involved.

There can be no catechesis without methodical organization which aims at transmitting revelation in all its fullness. The plan, however, should take into consideration the way in which adolescents think.

The adolescent already has some religious instruction and formation which stems from infancy through childhood up to his present stage of development. More active than passive in his reception of religious truths, he now aspires to a rediscovery. Those truths which he has previously learned he now wishes to embrace *personally*. The adolescent no longer feels satisfied by ideas alone and, conditioned by the times, seeks to have religious truths become a part of his own experience. It is only to this extent that they become meaningful to him. A certain progression of thought becomes evident in his makeup. In many ways, his thought process is closely allied to that of early childhood but differs rather deeply from adult thought and even from that of children ten to twelve years of age. There is here a sort of rebirth of knowledge, no longer spontaneous and imposed from without, as was the case before the age of seven, but more reflexive and autonomous. It is the age of discovery. The adolescent comes unexpectedly upon experiences and insights that lead to vast new horizons.

The essential characteristic of his knowledge is that it is guided in depth by voluntary and emotional impulses and impregnated by them to such an extent that one might say the adolescent has no thought and that he substitutes feelings for ideas. More specifically, the adolescent absorbs knowledge if the truth presented to him appears as a good, a value destined to shape his whole being permanently. This type of learning gives rise to certain necessary procedures in the development of a catechetical structure suitable for adolescents.

Catechetical instruction for adolescents must proceed according to what could be called a logical order, but of such a nature that it is by no means a purely intellectual, abstract approach. It is more a question of *logic based on the assent of a person to the values presented*. The whole person must be involved in what is presented and his personal reaction accounted for. The assent and adherence of the mind to the truths taught are won only if the whole being of the student is touched. Religious truths will then be accepted because they are geared to the aspirations of the adolescent who seeks the full accomplishment of his being in faith.[1]

During the catechetical discussions, then, the words of the catechist must be in permanent dialogue with the heart and the will which command the mind's assent. Take, for example, a catechesis on the Christian meaning of human love. There are two possible approaches.

A. The catechist may follow strictly logical, objective plan:
    love of concupiscence
    love of friendship
    grace and human love
    morality of love in Christ

This type of approach results in precise, objective knowledge, but it does not come to grip with the deep interests, the needs, or the will of the adolescent.

B. The catechist may proceed in quite another way, following a more concrete approach. He begins by discussing the aspirations, the searchings, and the failures of the young. Thus, from the very beginning, he seriously enters into dialogue with their interests and their burning issues. The discussion takes its starting point

---

1 When I was a young teacher in charge of the teaching of religion, I thought it essential to give my students a well-ordered lesson following a logical plan, with well-defined divisions and precise definitions. I am not saying now that all that is useless, but I have ceased to believe it is of prime importance. I remember being stopped in my tracks by one young man's remark: "Your lesson is very fine, but we are not with it." (Msgr. Tiberghien, quoted in *Lumen Vitae*)

from their vital situations; their personal needs are taken into consideration. Consequently they will find it most difficult not to become involved. The catechist is identified with them, so that when he speaks his words will be of value and carry weight.

In this discussion, the catechist vigorously expounds the purpose of love, again starting out from significant daily experiences. These experiences arouse the adolescent and stimulate a lively response because such experiences announce the message of love as a goal whose attainment brings happiness. This happiness is more than a pure ideal; it is concrete, realistic, and within the grasp of the individual. Thus presented, the truth about love becomes desirable, and the intellect embraces it.

In a word, the catechist gives a more profound presentation, showing how man achieves a fullness of love in and through Jesus Christ. This most important phase of the presentation must proceed from deepest conviction. Adolescents can sense very keenly any suggestion of insincerity which stems from halfheartedness or lack of conviction. This last phase, if it is to have any impact, must proceed from personal experience of the Christian mystery. On this last point the catechist meets the challenge that the adolescent proposes to him.

In this second perspective, the catechist treats practically the same subject as in the first, but in a different order and with different emphasis. There are, however, certain practical directives which should be taken into account for developing such a lesson.

1. The lesson plan should be flexible. Whatever the topic under study, the catechist must reach the basic preoccupations of the young. It is not a question of presenting God as the answer to man's aspirations. The message revealed must inaugurate a dialogue with those questions which the young person himself asks, which are to him most profound or disturbing. One way of achieving flexibility is to vary exposition of the topics under discussion so as to allow free days in the course of the lesson plan. During these times the students are encouraged to see the relevancy of what they are learning in catechesis to real-life situations, by reading novels, news reports, magazine articles, editorials, and the like. Exposition should not be straight lecture, but rather

dialogue and discussion, well prepared and leading to a clearly developed conclusion. This will, of course, include a presentation and explanation by the teacher of the subject under discussion.

Another possibility is to allow planned and progressive explanation of a lesson to be interrupted at times to treat of a subject which, because of interest aroused during the lesson, everyone wants to hear about. For example, something said during the catechist's presentation may spark observation on reading, friendship, confession, a national or local crisis.

2. The lesson plan must be developed methodically. Flexibility does not exclude the use of a well-thought-out plan. On the contrary, any digression, however necessary, is unprofitable if it does not return and relate to the main idea of the lesson for the day. It would be harmful if catechesis proceeded without some precise objective. Adolescents have ingenious ways of diverting a discussion and turning a dialogue into a general conversation or a monologue, ultimately pointless.

3. The lesson plan obviously must take adolescent interests into account. Very often a catechesis centers upon questions or problems of no concern to the adolescent: questions he never asks, problems that do not mean anything to him at this time. How should one draw up a plan in line with the interests and experiences of young people? Here are some suggestions which each catechist can adapt to his own needs and circumstances.

a. Speak first in terms of happiness and values before speaking in terms of duties and truth.[2] For example, in a lesson on the dignity of work, first present the dynamic and progressive aspects of work, then the problems and difficulties entailed in the life of the worker, and, finally, the moral implications.

b. Announce first the goal of Christian living, its final term, its destiny, before teaching the ways which lead there. Thus, treat of final glory before grace, of the "precious pearl" of the kingdom before the Beatitudes, which are conditions for arriving at the kingdom of heaven. This approach appeals not only to the

---

2 At least link duty and happiness, as Christ does in the Beatitudes.

intelligence of the pupils but also elicits a response from the will.

c. Speak first in the language of symbols or figures of speech and of fact before speaking in scientific terms, which are more conceptual and abstract. For example, first speak of grace in terms of friendship and of a happy life, and then use more technical terms—supernatural life, alliance, the gift of God's life in us, indwelling of the Spirit. Too often, catechesis reflects the subtleties and defensive techniques of a decadent scholasticism. This leads to a very impressive monologue, having very little relevance to the lives of the students. However, language, symbols, and concrete examples must be well within the grasp of the adolescent. Thus, what is said should provide a taste for the Christian way of life and find a resounding echo in human experience. Christ spoke as a Hebrew, to the men of His time, in the language of their day. Is this not the very pedagogy of the Gospels?[3] Should not the catechist speak to the adolescent in his time in language meaningful to him?

d. It follows, then, that the catechist should approach any catechetical theme by means of a concrete experience through which the young are more likely to discover interest and meaning. For example, the teacher knows about death through the actual experience of sickness, misfortune, or the loss of a friend.[4] From this same experience he can proceed to speak of the consolation of the Sacrament of the Sick for ailing or dying Christians, of the grace of the last anointing and its consolations. In fact, it is in such a time of trial as sickness or death that adolescents are strongly tempted to revolt against God. They may prefer to try to get along without Him and to give in to their natural inclination to withdraw within themselves. How wonderful then would it be for the catechist to enable Jesus Christ to come to them, that at such time Jesus Christ should come to give them back peace, goodness, strength, and forgiveness!

---

3 The will, the heart, and the emotions are thus Christianized. Adolescence is the ideal period for such evangelization.

4 The experience of death can also serve as an introduction to a lesson on the end of the world.

4. A plan must converge on a central theme. It should now be evident that every individual religion class, as well as every series of lessons, must converge on a central theme. The theme provides the source of the basic unity of all the discussions; it constitutes the primary axis of synthesis. Thus the examples which we have just given concerning the moral and spiritual life revolve about a fundamental idea: that of a call addressed to the heart of man so that he may be saved and achieve the plenitude of life by accepting Christ, the Man-God, Savior of the world. "Jesus Christ, dead and risen, saves us and calls us to the fullness of life in God." It would be good if all catechesis were each year organized around a central theme, a principle of synthesis. Thus the students would assimilate key ideas and points of reference, around which the various aspects of the program might crystalize. A haphazard program of catechesis creates an atmosphere of indifference and confusion. A change in the lead idea the following year renews interest and enriches the Christian vision; for instance, at fourteen: great plans; at fifteen: a people on the march towards Jesus Christ; at sixteen: towards life under the impulse of the Spirit.

5. The plan must constitute the key to the entire course. To satisfy the curiosity of the young and to whet their appetite, it would be good to announce at the beginning of each year, of each semester, and even at the start of each newly chosen topic of catechesis, the main ideas of the plan. This should include the questions to be treated in terms of the point of view chosen at the outset. Adolescents need and welcome such clear direction. They appreciate a course that is ordered and well organized.

6. The plan must not be too long. No good teacher ever lets a subject drag. This is most important for the catechist to keep in mind. A fourteen-year-old girl suggested that we should not treat "in a heavy manner a subject already worn out." Repetition is the mother of good studies unless it is deadened by "sameness," monotony, and needless restatement. Three to six discussions on a particular catechetical theme, even on a theme such as freedom, is ordinarily enough for adolescents. The catechist must certainly delve into the real questions which arise out of religious instruction and treat them profoundly and in detail, but he must be careful not to overdo it. Flexibility is here warranted as common sense dictates. But it is preferable to leave the adolescent not quite satisfied and let him want more. When we are studying temptation, the interest of the class may focus on Satan. This interest is normal, and the catechist should devote one class period to Satan. But he should certainly not spend two months on the theme of temptation.

IV. The catechist conducts discussion according to effective technique so indispensable in the formation of a free and responsible person. Sound technique in discussion enables the students to respond, to express their personality.

To be arresting and effective, the discussion should be based on logic adapted to the students mentality and on a number of pedagogical principles.

Not the least important of these principles is that the discussion should begin with something which fosters a personal bond between the catechist and the adolescent.

One of the most frequently reiterated ideas in polls taken among adolescents is that catechesis have some bearing on students' lives. To set up the necessary condition of empathy between teacher and students, the discussion takes its inspiration from the vital situation of youth. The teacher brings his catechesis to bear upon the hopes, aspirations, and needs of *this* group, living in *this* city at *this* particular phase in the development of *this* society. Too often the catechist prepares his discussion for the "ideal" adolescent, who does not really exist, and thus completely bypasses the real adolescent seated before him. Catechesis should be an authentic dialogue between teacher and pupils, and it should entail a collaboration both intellectual and practical. This principle merely confirms what every catechist should already know. To reach adolescents, the catechist must of necessity create a two-way exchange, personal and real, between himself and the young people. Moreover, to spark the discussion, the catechist should select rather ordinary events which constitute the warp and woof of the daily life of his students.

For example, taking account first of the theme of a series of lessons, as well as the aim of one particular lesson—the one at hand—the catechist could start off with an episode from a movie, a TV show, a popular song, or a magazine article which all have probably just seen, heard, or read. This movie, episode, or song must have a clear relation to the point which is to be the core idea of the lesson. By showing awareness and understanding of concrete and ideal things in the students' experience, the catechist is on their side; he is with them; he shares their lives. This leads to the first objective in setting up any class discussion, namely, to create a certain community of life between the catechist and the adolescent. Stimulating intellectual curiosity is secondary to the need for creating interpersonal human exchange. For this reason, the beginning of a discussion should be extremely personal, spontaneous, and varied. The catechist should certainly speak at times of himself, his own experiences, his religious and practical concerns. This often opens up the student, freeing him from those inhibitions which may make him reluctant to take a real part in the community experience of the class.

Dramatic stories which the catechist or the adolescent wants to feel, unless they establish a real relationship between the catechist and the life of the adolescent, should never take precedence over the more commonplace but more factual accounts of everyday happenings.

V. The catechist develops discussion so as to stimulate active progress in understanding and in faith.

Despite valid content, many religion lessons become tiresome simply because the adolescents accept the content passively. They receive the revealed message like something ready-made. Is it perhaps because certain methods of preparing for examinations have induced this intellectual lethargy? Is too much emphasis placed on learning definitions and formulas in the teaching of religion? Is it the catechist's task to put ready-made truths into students' heads while bypassing their hearts? Admittedly one does not invent truth. But Christ does present truth in such a way as to force man to search for it. He never presents it as something apart from Him, ready-made, dropped down from heaven neatly packaged, and ready for storage. He makes of man, so to speak, the creator of its discovery. Consider, for example, Christ's method with the Samaritan woman and with Nicodemus. (See John 4:1-42; 3:1-21.) Here were two people searching for truth, with Christ gradually opening it up to them from within. Each was actively engaged in the search. However, the truth had to have personal meaning to their lives. The truth is not a soporific. It is a goad. How can the catechist arrive at an active method of imparting Christian truth? Here are some practical directives.

1. Climate of mutual understanding. It is almost axiomatic that with adolescents no active discovery is made, no dialogue is initiated without a climate of mutual understanding, of profound communion between themselves and the catechist. A spirit of comradeship and of sincerity must reign in class. In view of this it is advisable that the teacher establish himself on a first-name basis with all his students. An effective method of initiating an atmosphere of community is to ask each student, in the first meeting of the class, to stand up and give his name, address, former school, and interests.

Do not irritate the students with hard-and-fast procedures and sanctions. Remember that this is *not* a language or a mathematics class and that the same pedagogical principles do not apply. Teachers of other subjects have to reconcile themselves to a very difficult adjustment in the teaching of religion. Do not antagonize group leaders; rather, try to be on their side, to have a positive faith in what is best in them, to give them responsibilities which create a cooperative spirit. For example, let a student interview someone, and then relay his information to the whole class; let another bring recordings or interesting documents. Some of the best discussions are those conducted by the students themselves. When the atmosphere becomes tense, reading from a book or playing a record is not a waste of time. Rather, it gives the student release from the purely academic and expands the dimensions of the catechetical presentation.

2. Climate of inquiry and research. Discussions should take the form of active inquiry and research along with the adolescents rather than the propounding of a thesis. Let the catechist be one with his class in searching for answers. Such is the secret of dynamic teaching. Begin with a concrete fact familiar to everyone. Then, swiftly, throw a new light on it, recall an experience which upsets the accustomed pace. Force the student to recognize himself, to reflect, to dream perhaps. Then ask the questions which he confusedly asks himself in secret. Let the catechist, with him, experience insecurity, even anxiety. Questions and research will help the student to emerge with the teacher into the light. This is in perfect consonance with adolescent psychology. The adolescent's greatest concern is himself. If the teacher can get him to come to grips with an understanding of himself, then he disposes him to become involved in the Christian mystery.

Take, for example, the sacrament of Penance. Beginning with a concrete fact, describe *first* the fear and shame one senses at the thought of confession. Agree that this is *normal*. The catechist feels the same way as the students do. We would like to be without defects, and we also long for our childhood innocence. *Then*, in dialectical opposition to this, quote St. John: "If we say that we have no sin, we deceive ourselves, and the truth is not in us" (1 John 1:8). Assert that we are all sinners, a fact common to the whole human race. Quote Christ's words to the sinners of yesterday and today: "It is not the healthy who need a physician, but they who are sick. I have not come to call the just, but sinners, to repentance" (Luke 5:31-32). The catechist must enable the words of Christ to make a deep impression. They must be presented forcefully. The words of Christ must be presented so that the students may clearly see their application in present-day situations. Skillful use of photographs for illustration can often achieve this aim. Let the examples given lead the students to stand before Christ, who knows man. Finally, when they have acknowledged their sinfulness before Christ, again ask the question, "Yet X is ashamed of going to confession. Why?"

This emergence into the light constitutes a challenge. The Christian experience is not something that can be taught, but something each individual must find for himself; its discovery has to be the term of a search; the kingdom of God must be sought.

If the catechist accomplishes this objective, he may be sure he has been relevant, and the pupils will say, as one young man said of his religion professor: "What is tremendous about his course is that we all feel involved. When he speaks, he reaches each person in the class . . . ; at the end of the class, we find that a common spirit has been established among us."

3. Rules for active dialogue. The catechist is constantly concerned with the students' fundamental interests. Avoid the error common to many textbooks: an initial, well-chosen, psychological contact, followed by a doctrinal "capsule" presented in itself and in an abstract way. The art of teaching consists in discovering the point of view from which the *mystery* will become *Good News* for the heart of man. This is the essential task of the catechist. Men must be able to see how the message of Jesus Christ is the relevant answer to their most basic needs. One must discover either the element in the Gospel which constitutes a problem disturbing man's present situation, or which meets one of his deeply felt needs. The message will then have direct relevance to the human condition. The catechetical discussion must be such that it constantly awakens a living dialogue with the interests of adolescents. The pedagogy of the dialogue involves the following constants:

a. The catechist must relate. At the start, the catechist manifests interest in the life of the man of today, for example, "What is the Church for us? Does the Church mean anything to us? To what extent do we participate in the life of the Church? Is it just a question of external membership?"

b. The catechist must disturb. The catechist carefully faces doubts or raises questions by showing the limitations and errors of the natural human position, for example, the feeling of dissatisfaction and discomfort some people experience in the Church. Conversely, imagine the world without the Church. Without the Gospel, life really has very little meaning. It would seem to be an insidiously cruel joke. And yet, it is only the challenge of Jesus Christ that can really prevent us from reverting to atheistic existentialism. Without Christ our logical stand can only be one of the most profound and soul-wracking despair which staggers our equilibrium.

c. The catechist must proclaim the Message. The catechist proclaims salvation as Good News, as a response to man's questionings and needs, reaching far beyond his expectations. The Gospel must be seen then as providing for the most basic of man's needs, as the very norm of his existence. Jesus Christ, the Resurrection and the Life, must not only snatch man from receding into a sickening darkness but also enable him to reach his fulfillment.

d. The catechist must expound the Message. After the kerygmatic announcement, the catechist develops the Message in terms of coherence and of contemporary living. This technique of the dialogue will take the shape of *two main forms of dialectic or organized presentation.*

Form 1. Antithesis

The catechist points out three contrasting terms:

What seems to be	*What will be*	*What is*
Human aspirations	The kerygmatic announcement of the Message	Light on the actual fact of behavior
EXAMPLE: The Church as the world sees it; various ways of looking at the Church; aspiration toward unity in the human community.	EXAMPLE: The heavenly Jerusalem.	EXAMPLE: The embryonic Church constantly developing and evolving; the Church in pilgrimage.

OR:

The Human Situation	*The Evangelical Proclamation*	*The Consequences*
One presents a situation of human existence, or brings to light a human experience.	Frequently noting its transcendence, one addresses the Good News of this human situation or experience.	One shows what the Gospel brings to the human situation or experience; how the Gospel modifies it or surpasses it.
EXAMPLE: How a man prepares for his future	EXAMPLE: How God takes care of us actively (Providence)	EXAMPLE: How a man who believes in Providence prepares for his future

Form 2. Progression by successive development

The catechist passes by stages from the question posed to a discovery of the answers, whether it is a question expressed progressively or a reality discovered in successive phases. In both cases, he starts from the level closest to experience, that is, the level closest to the young person's affective life and to his intellectual capacity (sense intuition by way of parables). The question posed is then clarified by a more sophisticated elaboration. For example, before mentioning grace as supernatural life, the catechist speaks of a vacation experience, then of a friendship which changed our life, and so on. Such an approach must keep in mind the listeners' stage of psychological development. It also presupposes familiarity and understanding of the teen-age world which escapes so many adults. The notional elaboration not only supposes the catechist to be conversant with traditional and contemporary theology, but, more important, his ability to make it applicable to the concete situation from which the discussion takes it inspiration. The discussion must be prepared carefully and discussed skillfully.

On each level, interest must be awakened anew by awakening the desire to discover what follows or by explicitly posing questions which every man asks himself implicitly.[5] It is important to channel the interest awakened in the adolescent. If it is allowed to wander aimlessly without any direction, the student will lose interest in the question and confidence in the catechist.

4. **The catechist must promote the development of ideas.** One of the most effective means of securing active intellectual involvement consists in proposing *concrete activities* which coincide with the various phases of the lesson and which necessitate the students' personal effort and reflective comprehension during

---

5 In using one or the other of these two types of plan, it is important to use concrete language, to speak in a manner which will awaken an echo in the young person's experience of life. This is a question of approach, of words and titles. While avoiding excess, the catechist should choose words and expressions corresponding to concrete reality or at least capable of evoking true spiritual realities. For example, the "child of God" is well-worn. Why not use "people of God"?

each phase of the discussion. This can be done in two ways:

a. Suggest intellectual activities in preparation for the various ideas evoked in discussion. The whole point is to find interesting things to do, at each step of the progression, in order to provoke a reaction or involvement on the part of the student.

Ask a question requiring an explicit answer. "Do you sometimes think of your future?"—"What, in your opinion are the responsibilities of a high-school student at home?"

Have a student write on the chalkboard. Have a student give a summary of the discussion, and allow him to ask for comments. Show pictures and photographs from newspapers and magazines. Ask for concrete facts to illustrate ideas expressed. Ask a student to present relevant articles from magazines or selections from books, and allow him to involve the entire class in comment.

The teacher often resorts to his own initiative and experience to provide a variety of activities. However, a teacher never feels that it is *his* responsibility to entertain the class. Quite the contrary, he achieves very satisfactory results by proposing and allowing the students to accept the responsibility of conducting activities. By trying to take everything into their own hands, teachers often ignore the talents and capabilities of students.

b. Provide for moments of introspection, of reflection on past experience, which will serve as starting-points for deducing intellectual truths. The catechist is counting here on the adolescent's need to feel, to experiment, to commit himself affectively before assenting to a proposition of the intellectual order. The whole point consists in providing a true-to-life situation in which the adolescent will involve himself affectively,[6] and then to have him discover, by analysis and reflection, the intellectual proposition or the religious message implied in this form of experience. A vivid description of the funeral of a great man, a Christian, focusing on the impact of his death upon his widow, would provide an experience leading to deep reflection upon a profound religious

---

6 Very often, through a story, an event, or an analogy, the adolescent can be made to undergo an emotional experience vicariously and to analyze it. Nothing sparks serious reflection so well as the example of a good person with whom the adolescent identifies.

truth. As a wife, what did she endure? As a woman of faith, what was she thinking? Reflection upon this experience serves to introduce catechesis on the meaning of death.

In this perspective, experience precedes thought, and thought arises from reflection on experience. In catechesis, the Message is grasped at the precise moment when the adolescent analyzes and measures what, in his own life, is affected by the Message. *Thus the Message is grasped, not through the enunciation of a verbal proposition concerning a certain truth, but by its consequences on human life.* Is this not a truly biblical pedagogy? God did not reveal Himself through the presentation of a thesis, but through the experience which, each day, the Hebrew people acquired of His presence and of His action. The prophets' role was to have the people reflect on this experience and announce its significance. This development of thought, leaning constantly on experience, is very rich and effective. Yet, it is not without some difficulties. It risks violating the freedom of students by leading them to excessive introspection which might result in self-centeredness. At this age most young people are conscious enough of profound and disturbing effects, psychological and physiological, within them. There is also the danger of creating too emotional an atmosphere and of confusing religious experience with Christian faith. The prudent catechist is careful to avoid these pitfalls.

c. The catechist must ever bear in mind these considerations: The revealed Message does not flow from intellectual effort; it is a witness, a proclamation, an announcement from above, not a fruit of human activity.

Only if a subject is brought to a consideration of his personal human situation in view of the faith will the student achieve a true understanding of the Message. The catechist, however, avoids exploiting the adolescent's budding liberty by the compelling experiences or attendant reflections proposed to him in the course of discussion.

The affective atmosphere must be tempered so as to avoid sentimentality and exaggerated identifications. At a later age, teenagers tend to resent sentimentality, and there is always a danger of throwing the baby out with the bath water.

In order to be truly and seriously catechical, the discussion ought to end with a clearly expresed verbal statement which will fix in the mind and the memory the experience made in faith. Certain educators are tempted to remain on the affective level. It is very easy to allow this affective method to become an end in itself so that the very goal of the discussion is never really achieved and the students feel a certain disappointment when they finally do not reach it.

VI. The catechist enlivens discussion by recalling personal experiences and current events.

Adolescents expect the discussion in the religion class to be of vital concern. "The lessons should be exciting, the explanations well-presented; the teacher should give many vivid examples."— "If the topic is boring, the teacher ought to make it appealing, meaningful to all, and relevant to the facts of everyday life." The degree of vitality will be assured only by reference to personal experiences and to current events.

1. **Personal experience.** The catechist does not fear to bear witness, to reveal Christianity as it is living in him, to share his reactions, for example, to a headline news story, a TV program, a human encounter. This procedure usually prompts a lively rapport with the students. A sixteen-year-old-boy said, "We like the teacher to give factual examples from his own life describing his ecumenical activities." An account which includes episodes involving personal experience will usually be effective provided that the teacher has established a strongly interpersonal relationship with his students.

From time to time, talks given by qualified outsiders will carry great weight. A unit on the Mass might start with a talk on its meaning by a young lay man or woman of a nearby parish: "What the Mass means to me." Or again, a lesson on the role of the theater in Christian life might be discussed by a producer or a director, especially if a film club is active in the school. A psychologist's reflections or the nature of religious commitment could be a valuable contribution to catechetical discussion.

2. **Current events.** The catechist ought to refer constantly to cur-

rent events, and often exploit news stories featured in *Life, Time, Look, U.S. Catholic, Ave Maria,* and other magazines. It is not a matter of appearing well-informed, but of helping adolescents to read with the eye of faith about the daily events which affect their lives. It enables them to extend their horizons beyond their own neighborhood and locale. They become aware of the desperate problems of war, hunger, ignorance, and social injustice which countless people must face. They are challenged to put the world's burning issues into a Christian perspective.

Reference to personal experience and to current events is not a pedagogical gimmick. It is an expression of Christian charity, seeking to reach the lives of our young people. Beyond being a method of making the religion class lively, it is life itself, the life of every day, face to face with eternal life. The catechist should enable his students to see that Christianity is not confined to only one compartment or our lives but that it takes on a whole new dimension enveloping every facet of our lives.

VII. The catechist provides formal structure for his catechesis.

A catechesis which takes into account all the necessary psychological factors and, consequently, maintains a profitable dialogue with adolescent interests, runs the risk of neglecting to give the student an intellectual structure, and so becoming untrue to the intellectual dimension of the student. As far as possible, the catechist keeps his religious teaching within a solid framework of clear formulation.

For this purpose, it is good to end a catechetical discussion with summaries, clear definitions, precise formulas, and even with diagrams. However, these techniques must be used moderately, or else the sense of mystery, which is difficult enough to establish and maintain, is lost in a maze of involved definitions and subtle formulas. The danger is minimized if the catechist uses these formulas sparingly during the discussions but frequently *at the end* to give a precise structure to his thought.[7]

---

7 The teacher may find summaries in textbooks helpful for memorization. But a synthesis should constitute the end-point of catechesis, not the whole lesson.

VIII. The catechist makes the lesson itself an aid to memorization.

It is generally difficult to have adolescents memorize formulas by rote, unless they are helped to do so by group pressure and a favorable classroom atmosphere. High-school students generally associate memorization of formulas with the teaching procedure of elementary schools, and for that reason they resent it in a religion class. Memorization, therefore, is achieved by indirect methods.

1. Before introducing a subject, the teacher writes the plan on the chalkboard in colored chalk. The students generally appreciate an organized presentation. It fosters confidence in the teacher.

2. During the religion class, he could dictate a short résumé of each section as he explains it. This procedure often assists in the maintenance of discipline. Prolonged discussion often leads the students to become noisy and restless. The dictated résumé re- stores silence and the atmosphere of study.

3. At the end of class, the teacher could dictate definitions provided that these are meaningful and relevant, that is, thoroughly understood by the student.

4. From time to time, the students could repeat certain formulas in order to commit them to memory. The beginning of each period could serve as a time to recall the essential points discussed in the previous religion class.

5. The teacher could ask questions, distribute written questionnaires, or carry on selected activities aimed at developing precise formulas. The formula is always a point of synthesis, not of deduction or analysis. Most textbooks provide ample review material.

IX. The catechist varies the form of discussion.

These practical suggestions regarding the pedagogy involved in a catechetical presentation need not confine the catechist to inflexible regimentation, stifling all personal initiative. Rigidity would be a betrayal of the Church's pedagogy, which uses various teaching methods. Variety in Christian teaching is more effective to express doctrinal objectivity and to convey the Message in its full extent. Monolithic methodology would be a betrayal of the charisma proper to each catechist, a charisma he must take into account if he is to obey the Spirit. Such rigidity would even be contrary to the adolescent mentality, which requires variety in teaching. Variety in the style of presentation is essential to equilibrium in catechesis. There are four types of presentation.

1. The Dialogue

In this method, the teacher assumes the attitude of the listener who helps the adolescent to express his deepest thoughts and, in so doing, to deepen his thinking. Such exchanges must intervene from time to time to reduce tension, to stimulate curiosity, and to link the young to one another and to the catechist. They will also serve to maintain the direction of the discussion and to introduce new catechetical themes. The dialogue can be carried out either in writing or orally.

A. In Writing

For example, before studying the Mass, pass out a short anonymous questionnaire. "What is the Mass to you?"—"Certain lay people go to Mass every day. Why, in your opinion?" The problems thus discovered will be aired in common, but anonymity is always respected.[8] At other times, one can ask the students to bring to class newspaper clippings and documents relating to the theme that is being discussed.

B. Orally

It is desirable to resort often to oral discussion. The adolescent is asked to express his objections to a certain aspect of religion or to comment on his friends' attitudes. If the group is small, he may

---

8 Short questionnaires are useful, but abuse of them annoys and even antagonizes students.

write all the opinions given on the chalkboard. Sort them out; sift out essentials from accidentals.[9]

Insist right from the start that the class listen attentively and seriously to ideas expressed by any fellow student. Teach the pupils to ask precise questions, to avoid rude answers, and to listen to answers without causing disorder.

A Christian educator acquires the art of asking and answering questions with kindness. Adolescents appreciate kindness more than anything else. A teacher, however, is firm in maintaining order. Sarcasm is especially resented by a teen-ager. It has no place in a religion class. The catechist does not allow a noisy atmosphere to be created in which adolescents will not listen to one another. This point is very important, yet often neglected. The teacher must acquaint himself with the rules which govern group dynamics.

The type of session here described requires of the teacher great skill, even a special charisma. He does not delay over irrelevant questions, nor does he dodge more academic yet real problems.

2. The Formal Lesson

Catechesis aims both at enlightening the mind and at influencing behavior. Therefore, the teacher blends practical considerations with formal reflections. Constant reference is made to questions which are of crucial concern to adolescents.

Consider, for example, the following approaches to the sacrament of Penance.

1ST THEME: *We are all sinners.* Refer to the guilt feeling experienced by adolescents and to the difficulty they find in admitting their sins in confession. The teacher proceeds carefully here because adolescents often refuse to admit to any feelings of guilt.

2ND THEME: *Penance, sacrament of God's pardon and of man's conversion.* The catechist here reaffirms the primacy

---

9 In discussion with adolescents, it is of great importance to summarize periodically, to draw attention to the main ideas, and to do so very precisely. Otherwise, the discussion becomes too vague.

of God's merciful action in contrast to the oppressive-
ness of the young person's guilt feelings.

3RD THEME: *Confession to a priest.* Why tell one's sins to a priest?
This classical objection serves as starting point for an
explanation of the priest's role as mediator. Man
needs sensible signs. In the sacrament of Penance he
is presented with a sign that demands a heart-to-heart
encounter.

4TH THEME: *Is it necessary to go to confession?* Discuss why.

5TH THEME: *Confession rebuilds man.* Discuss how.

This type of presentation is well adapted to adolescent psychology. It corresponds directly to the adolescent's need for self-as-
sertion. The student should also be permitted to see the extensive
equilibrium—social, psychological, and moral—which is restored
to the individual who has made his peace with God and his neighbor in the sacrament of Penance.

3. The Biblical Approach

In this type of lesson, the catechist persuasively proclaims the
realities of the kingdom of God with a view to conversion. This is
not done with terminology which, although clear and exciting for
adults, has very little meaning for a boy or girl. The intense moments of conversion must not be overdone, as young people have
a limited capacity of reacting to them. A catechist realizes that an
adolescent is hardly capable of the total commitment which is
strived for in adult catechesis. Many disappointing experiences
can be avoided by keeping this fact in mind.

4. The Intellectual Approach

The importance of ending each lesson with a precise conclusion
has been previously stressed. There is room, therefore, for a style
of approach providing more firmness of structure and promoting
ease in memorization.

Keeping in mind the nuances established above, the catechist
varies his method of approach so that strong presentations alternate with relatively relaxing periods.

B

X. The catechist varies the method for class prayers.

Two precautions should be taken:

1. Avoid always beginning and ending with a prayer as though prayer were the way to call the class to order.

2. Avoid using prayer that is too personal, too pointedly linked with class discussion. Impersonal prayer is necessary at this stage to respect interior freedom.

Vary the style and time of prayer. Use Biblical readings, liturgical texts, traditional formulas. In certain classes, let the students take the initiative. Any method is excellent as long as it does not become burdensome.

II. Outline and Analysis of Catechesis for Adolescents

This active catechesis on Divine Providence illustrates principles and suggestions presented and discusssed in preceding pages of this section. It is taken from a program of religious education drawn up by teams of THE GRAIL, an international movement of young women working on all six continents in every field of the lay apostolate of the Church.[1]

Catechesis on Divine Providence

THEME	God cares for us.
AIM, PURPOSE, AND DOCTRINAL GUIDANCE	To open the mind of the adolescent to a living faith in Divine Providence.
	To show the adolescent, through reflection on experience, how the truth of God's Providence concerns the whole direction of human life.
	To deduce from these aims:
	1. what God's Providence is,
	2. how Providence modifies our human condition.

1 *Grail Youth Leadership Program, 1959.* The Grail Religious Education Department, 208 Clinton Avenue, Brooklyn, New York 11205, U. S. A. Parts of the original catechesis have been adapted, and the general development has been summarized.

PREPARATION

TEXT

What do you think of the future? Do you spend much time thinking about it? Do you sometimes worry about it? (A few facts drawn from experience will help young people to recognize their misgivings concerning the future.) The fact that we are Christians, that we believe in Christ—how does this fact affect our misgivings, our worries, our plans?

It is difficult to pledge one's future, to make a commitment. The future often seems to loom before us as a threat. Anxiety for the morrow affects us deeply and even painfully.

In order to make right decisions, one needs to know the facts. Today (this evening), let us examine the facts with which you are concerned:

What do you know about yourself?

What makes *you* different from others?

Name some of the characteristics that distinguish you from others.

Physical features
Talents
Interests
Circumstances
Limitations

ANALYSIS

Question ...

From the very beginning of the catechesis, there should be deep involvement in the problems of the adolescent. The catechist identifies himself with his hearers. The basic question is stated, but the answer is not yet clear. There is anxiety concerning the future. How does God fit into our misgivings?

Reflection ...

Appeal to affective experience.

An experiment is proposed for planning the future. Observe that this experiment is attractive. It concerns the basic interests of the adolescent: the building of his personality and of his future. The adolescent will be provided with all the helps needed to see how he should organize his life.

It is to be noted that, in the beginning, this projection is built up without explicit reference to God. This is very important if we are to understand the subse-

Family
Friends
Environment
Education
Experience
Personality

quent educational development of the adolescent. As a matter of fact, it is during a second stage that it will be possible to educe strong evidence to show what Providence contributes as compared with what is derived from natural factors or human experience.

Have members of the class list the points above on the chalkboard. Discuss each point in order to find out how each series of experiences, of situations, of aptitudes goes to make each person *one of a kind*.

Activity . . .

The young people are asked to discover the elements and factors which go to make up the future. They are asked to write on the chalkboard. The young people are asked to provide examples of each of the constituent elements. Thus, the adolescent becomes deeply involved and strongly committed to participation in collective action.

Family: An eldest girl whose mother dies and who must, in consequence, take on greater responsibility; the effect on her in a large family, in a small family.

Experience: Someone has seen a person, or even an animal, die; an experience like that of Anne Frank.

Environment: rich or poor, happy or sad; how this factor affects a person.

Friends: An experience of deep friendship may make a person more friendly to others.

Talents: various kinds of talent—
Social: noticing a person who is not feeling well; being able to cheer people up.
Intellectual: knowing one's convictions and holding fast to

them; seeing another's good points rather than his bad ones; readiness and ease in understanding; desire for knowledge. Practical: knowing how to sew, to plan a party, to keep one's clothes tidy.

And now, draw a picture of yourself, taking into consideration all these elements: family, talents, acquired experience . . . Think only of yourself. Sum up the facts that concern *you*. (Period of silence for writing in personal notebooks)

A call for self-examination. At this point the adolescent is induced to turn his search inwards, to apply it to himself.

PRESENTATION

You have just had a preview, an imaginary picture of your future. And God? What has He to do with this?

Study of the question is resumed with a new approach in view.
In the Preparation, two purposes have been achieved:

1. The young people have become interested. They have succeeded in planning their future, both collectively and individually, but without any reference to God.

2. Thanks to his way of speakings, of his identifying himself with the concerns of his young audience, the catechist will be deeply linked with them. When he speaks, what he says will have a deep and lasting effect.

God takes active care of you. Hear how God speaks to man, to the man who worries and dreams about his petty plans:

Catechetical announcement . . . After this involvement in depth, the catechist is going to announce the revealed Message. The young

B*

To Abraham, hesitating before the road of the future: "Walk in my presence . . ." (Genesis 17:1). This means: "Do not be afraid. I am with you."

Through the Psalmist: "Though father and mother forsake me, yet will the Lord accept me" (Psalms 26.10). This means, "I shall not abandon you." To a people walking in fear in the desert of life, the sacred writer says of God: "He found them in a wilderness, a wasteland of howling desert. He shielded them and cared for them, guarding them as the apple of his eye. As an eagle incites its nestlings forth by hovering over its brood, so he spread his wings and bore them up on his pinions" (Deuteronomy 32:10-11).

Lastly, in still more wondrous fashion, God knows us so well, God stays so close to us that He comes precisely to share our human destiny, our human future, in order that we may have our share in His future destiny as Son of God. Who now would dare to be afraid? Who could dare have doubts about his future, his success, or his talents?

Jesus speaks: "Look at the birds of the air: they neither sow nor reap nor gather into barns, and yet your heavenly Father feeds them . . . And why are you anxious about clothing? Consider the lilies of the field, how they grow; they neither toil nor spin; yet I tell you, even Solomon in

people have just gone through the experience of planning the future "without God." Now, in a forceful manner, the catechist proclaims the truth of the Providence of God, which almost directly opposes this experience. It upsets the purely human forecast of life. In order to be concrete and striking, this announcement must first of all be biblical. The announcement, as we see, is like a seed that falls on soil that has been prepared and cultivated. Nevertheless, this announcement is such, in its somewhat general and positive form, that the young person is unable, at first, to understand the connection between his former experience and the word of God. The young person's misgivings about the future, his worries, his merely human values and projects are challenged, questioned, discussed, and overruled. From a clash of opinions springs the light of truth.

all his glory was not arrayed like one of these. But if God so clothes the grass of the field, which to-day is alive and tomorrow is thrown into the oven, will he not much more clothe you, O men of little faith? Therefore, do not be anxious, saying, 'What shall we eat?' or 'What shall we drink?' or 'What shall we wear?' For the Gentiles seek all these things; and your heavenly Father knows that you need them all. But seek first his kingdom and his right-eousness, and all these things shall be yours as well. Therefore do not be anxious about tomor-row, for tomorrow shall be anx-ious for itself. Let the day's own trouble be sufficient for the day" (Matthew 6:26, 28-34).

St Augustine says: "God cares for us as if each were the sole object of His love, . . . and He cares for all as He does for each."

If we believe this, will it make a difference in our ideas of our-selves and of our future?

I remember a teacher who en-couraged one of his students to become a lawyer. This student had a keen mind. He was bril-liant, and he could express him-self with ease. However, he did

The question is posed again. But the question is only partially an-swered. What exact connection if there between the previous ex-perience (merely human organ-ization of one's life) and Pro-vidence (God's taking an active interest in our welfare)?

Catechetical explanation . . .
In response to the question, the catechist begins by using a strik-ing analogy, one closely related to the experience and the inter-ests of the adolescent. The ado-

not take his talent seriously. As an adult and competent educator, the teacher could see the young man's possibilities, what he was capable of becoming, far beyond any knowledge the young man could have of himself. Recognizing all the student's talents, the teacher made the young man realize his potentialities and his latent gifts. This is somewhat like God's way with us. He sees our possibilities far better than we do. He desires to have us become and He gives us the means of becoming that unique, broadened, and enriched person which we are potentially capable of being.

We are not finished products. What is going on within us? Think of yourselves as you were six years ago. Are you not somewhat different? We are often surprised at what we have been able to accomplish and what we have been able to become. We are somewhat like a seed which turns into a flower. Have you ever watched something grow, how it begins, what it turns into? (Seed, stalk, flower.) Just seeing the stalk, we should scarcely expect it to turn into a beautiful red or yellow flower. Yet it has within itself the power of becoming a particular flower, red or yellow, even when it is nothing more than a seed. And God knows, and God wills, and God

lescent has no difficulty seeing himself in the presence of his teacher.

Now, in a second analogy, the action of Providence is more fully described, and at the same time an indirect appeal is made to the adolescent to trust in God. It should be noted that assertion of belief in Divine Providence is very personal: it affects the adolescent and calls upon him to place his trust in God, to commit his future to God, and to be sure of his unknown possibilities because God is present, because Jesus Christ has made a covenant with man. This is our crowning glory, the tangible proof of God's Providence.

(The idea of Providence is explained in detail.)

Let us remember our first experiment in projecting our future succeeds beyond any stretch of the imagination.

It is all the more true in the case of men and women, since God cares so much for all of us that He sends His Son, Jesus Christ, to be with us always.

without reference to God. A great step forward has been taken, not only at the intellectual level, but in the realm of experience and reflection, perhaps even by a spiritual conversion. At this point, after the prophetic announcement, which is partly from within, the adolescent is led little by little to review his previous experience in the Christian perspective. It may even be said that it is through the vital consequences of the Message concerning the first experience that the adolescent is led to understand the exact significance of the Message itself.

CONCLUSION

Can you estimate how much Providence influences the ordinary happenings of human life and human worries about the future? God's care for us is boundless. His love for us is all-powerful. Providence is a relationship of infinitely intelligent and powerful Love which God has with all men. The object of this Love is victory without parallel (Christ). You have found your own answer: the person who builds his future on true Christian faith in Providence—knows that he possesses gifts and hidden possibilities which he may not yet see distinctly but in which he believes because of God's love for him; knows that even his handicaps and infirmities may have a

Discussion of the catechetical question is resumed.

The catechist answers the question himself, thus introducing a clear conclusion. The detailed explanation deals with the substance of the Message.

The explanation considers also the consequences of the Message in relation to human life.

The latter part of the conclusion might be carried out effectively by means of a collective questionnaire or a personal exercise.

On one hand, merely human reflections may be made:

—I am handicapped for life, crippled by disease; I am a poor, unfortunate character; I dread the future; I always have hard luck; and the like.

positive value because of God;
is certain of outstanding success;
places all his cares and worries
in the hands of the Lord and
steps forward with cinfidence.

PRAYER

O almighty God, eternal Father,
look upon each of us here today
(this evening), and grant us light
and faith to understand Your
care and interest in us. Amen.

The young people are then asked
to express a Christian reaction.

ANALYTIC SUMMARY

1. This catechesis, if not complicated, is somewhat lengthy. The catechist might simplify and adapt it to his audience. This model gives
   ample details in order to provide a thorough development of the main
   points of a discussion based on a dialectic for very lively dialogue.

2. Dialogue does not necessarily mean oral dialogue. Dialogues without
   words are often more effective. There is dialogue whenever there is
   interest and response.

3. The methodology analyzed above is not intended primarily as a
   guide for preparation of a catechesis. It is intended more as a help in
   the evaluation of a catechesis which has already been presented. The
   analysis outlines rules and principles for dialogue in catechesis.
   Dialogue, however, is a living reality which cannot be created merely
   by mathematical adherence to rules and laws. Rather it is the projection of a real, interpersonal exchange of ideas between the catechist
   and his audience.

PART TWO · *The Catechesis*

I. Catechesis of Adolescents

I. Classroom Atmosphere

1. Qualities adolescents look for in the catechist. The atmosphere of a religion class depends primarily upon the catechist. It cannot be created artificially by turning on a record player, using a movie projector, or simply giving orders and directions. It is conditioned by the religion teacher's personality. The students encounter Christ in the person of their teacher. In describing teachers they like, adolescents use words like "sympathetic" and "understanding." These words take on varying meanings according to different stages of psychological development. But what do they mean to adolescents? What qualities do adolescents look for in a religion teacher?

The characteristics they hope to find are nearness, dedication, prestige, and stability.

NEARNESS. Nearness is a quality of the heart. The teacher possessing it accepts and approaches the adolescent as a person and is keenly aware of the aspirations and ideas of the student. He enters into the student's life in such a way that the student becomes personally conscious of his interest. The adolescent feels that the teacher is on his side and is attuned to the same wavelength. If the catechist shows personal concern, then the adolescent feels at ease with him. "We can ask the teacher any question that bothers us."

DEDICATION. Students want teachers who are zealous and dedicated. They want teachers who speak with ardent love of Christ. They want religion to captivate and possess them. Religion has to make sense to them. It has to be vibrant and timely. Students look up to teachers who, though young at heart, maintain the dignity becoming their professional status. The exuberance of youth seeks inspiration from a teacher who is dynamically zealous.

PRESTIGE. In youngsters emerging somewhat fearfully and uncertainly from childhood, the teacher by his personality and way of acting has to encourage and foster self-fulfillment and openness. There is no place for a teacher who is maternalistic, for one who is apprehensive or diffident. Such a teacher stifles initiative and arouses hostility. Adolescents want a teacher who can lead, someone they can follow, someone who will guide them out of their child's world towards adulthood. Their teacher has to be an ideal, a hero to them.

Students will be impressed and influenced by a catechist with whom they have a feeling of mutual trust and confidence. A teacher's personal competence brings prestige to his religious instruction. He is intellectually alert to answer any questions adequately, thereby showing that religion can meet the challenges of the times. He establishes the link between religion, on the one hand, and science, modern discoveries, and world events on the other. He is open to opinions at variance with his own. His students feel free to express exactly what they think. The teacher is intellectually honest in suggesting solutions to difficult problems. His answers are based on knowledge and experience. He never resorts to dismissive flippancies or to weak, off-the-cuff remarks in order to cover up any deficiency in his professional preparation. Resort to such is incompatible with prestige.

Students recognize prestige in the competence of an up-to-date mind and of success in human affairs. Prestige undoubtedly presupposes certain natural qualities and adequate qualifications especially in the minds of young people who have not as yet closely encountered Christ in His Church. Prestige, however, rests on the teacher's sense of Christian values; it grows out of his interest, fidelity, and generosity in the service of youth.

STABILITY. Since the adolescent is still in large measure a child, the teacher has to provide and foster stability in the student's life. The adolescent does not like a teacher who changes his mind and his method with each class. He cannot respond to a teacher who is mercurial. He appreciates continuity in the teacher's approach and firmness in his demands. Yet, inasmuch as he already tends toward the subjective attitudes characteristics of adolescence, the adolescent needs someone who tempers continuity with a measure of versatility and imagination. To be self-assured in face of the confusing onrush of sensations and changes, the adolescent needs the steadying influence of a teacher who is stable yet flexible.

If the catechist is serious, confident, and self-possessed, then his students can appreciate and rely upon him. They will naturally see in him the goal of the development of their own personality. At the same time the catechist has to be flexible, available to the student's needs, open to current ideas and trends. He has to be a teacher who knows student tastes in music or teen-age fads and fashions and who is unperturbed by them. He has to be able to share in an adult way the interests and enthusiasms of teen-agers. He has to be one who is in tune with the times, one who loves and appreciates young people. A certain grace, a certain flexibility reveal in the teacher a sense of balance which helps the adolescent keep his footing in the midst of interior turmoil.

The adolescent finds himself being thrust into a world of new and confusing experiences. Confronted with many problems, the youth of today do not hesitate to pose questions unmentionable a generation ago. In discussing the problems of youth, the catechist should never rebuff honest inquiry and sincere curiosity. He should not be embarrassed or perplexed. "Let them tell us the facts of life without beating around the bush," a sixteen-year-old girl remarked of her teachers.

Young people, then, seek teachers who strike a happy balance of authority and companionship. They do not seek a scholarly pedagogue. They want a teacher who is firm but resilient; a teacher who proceeds with order and harmony, yet is able to adapt to the many situations which arise in religion classes. Such a teacher has style and self-assurance which give him pliability and availability. He has faith which makes him open and radiant. Such is the sympathetic and understanding catechist.

2. **Classroom atmosphere adolescents expect.** For adolescent instruction, the catechist is the most important factor in creating classroom atmosphere. He is the pacesetter. The effectiveness of his procedure depends upon talent and experience. Adolescents themselves, however, also constitute a determinant factor. What do they consider essential to a well-run class? From research done in this field, four conclusions emerge:

A. Adolescents want discipline. Among representative groups surveyed, 25 per cent of preadolescents (11-15 years), 22.5 per cent of adolescents (16-19), and 22 per cent of young adults (20-25) demanded discipline. Discipline, however, has different connotations with various age groups.

For preadolescents, discipline means simply avoiding noise, stopping chatter, keeping quiet, listening to the teacher. Discipline is order and calm. It is understood objectively. Responsibility for discipline lies chiefly with the teacher.

For adolescents, discipline is more closely linked with application to study. It is a matter of wanting to pay attention to the teacher rather than of merely being in religion class as an obligation. Discipline for this group takes on a more subjective, more active connotation. Responsibility for discipline is shared by both teacher and students.

Young adults have still a different notion. For them, discipline is not a matter of exterior attitude. Far from it. Discipline is an atmosphere of interior receptivity to religious teaching. Responsibility for discipline lies chiefly with the student and acts as a test of his maturity.

Preadolescents, then, see discipline as *silence*. "If everyone were silent and orderly, there would be no need for punishment," observes a thirteen-year-old.

Discipline depends upon order and organization which effectively channel youth's natural vitality and energy into productive activity. Children are quick to perceive disorganization in preparation or presentation and can hardly be expected to respond favorably. They become restless and unruly. "Make rules, set standards, form groups," is the way a group of eleven-year-old girls put it. Children like order and organization.

A few suggestions here on maintaining order and silence may be helpful to both beginning and experienced teachers.

Establish order and silence at the beginning of class. Do not tolerate infractions like boisterous talk or scrambling for seats.

During individual assignments, require not merely silence in word but absence of all other noise and disturbance. During group assignments, let students speak in a low voice and move about quietly when necessary.

Call the class to attention when whispering spreads or the volume of chatter rises. A general call to order spares individual feelings and restores quiet. At all times and at all cost, avoid sarcasm, to which children are extremely sensitive. Sarcasm hampers communication with an individual and may arouse resentment throughout the class.

Occasionally invite a talkative student to air his ideas before the class, and thus possibly turn a menace to discipline into an asset to class discussion.

Give the intractable troublemaker the choice of keeping silence or of leaving the class to report to the principal or supervisor. Use this dismissal only as a last resort in extreme instances. Always act and speak calmly, without unduly humiliating the offender.

Assign some purposeful and challenging catechetical activity to the student who compulsively tries to get attention by violating order and silence. Make this activity not merely punitive but corrective, creative, practical, and useful.

Do not remain angry after having imposed a penalty or taken other disciplinary measures. Rather let the class see you are confident that the refractory student will ultimately become an asset to the group. Use discipline to win over toublesome students, not to isolate them. Let the troublemaker be an object lesson to other potentially unruly students. Students readily appreciate justice and fairness in dealing with infractions of discipline.

Let the atmosphere of the religion be quiet but relaxed. Make it conducive to listening to the Word of God. Avoid subjecting adolescents to long periods of reflection. Here are some adolescent views on classroom atmosphere: "There must be openness." —"Everyone should feel at ease to speak as in a family."—"There should be a good spirit in the classroom."—"There has to be silence, but now and then we like a joke."—"We ought to be able to enjoy the religion class."

Discipline should be spontaneous rather than imposed. It should arise from a trusting student-teacher relationship initiated by the catechist. It should create a happy atmosphere, not one of constraint and tension. Discipline should nurture voluntary attention to God our Father, who speaks to the students in and through the lesson. Its source should be personal freedom joyfully exercised.

Obviously, creating such an atmosphere depends to a great degree upon the teacher's personality, ingenuity, and resourcefulness.

B. Adolescents want activity. While they expect order and discipline, adolescents like to be active in the religion class. God's message should be a real and vitally interior experience; they ought to relate to it more readily than to, say, mathematics or science. They want to take part in discussion and to do something specific through activities. Through discussion and activity they give to the Word of God their active response inspired by faith.

Adolescents feel that they take an active part in religion class if they can reveal their reactions and express their ideas. These typical student opinions are illuminating: "We want to experience the lesson, not endure it."—"Let students express their preference in choice of activities."—"Let us say what we think."—"Let the students supply the examples."

Students at times might be allowed even to decide upon class procedure. "Let all the pupils search for ideas on a subject, arrange and group them, and thus furnish interesting topics for study and discussion." In assuming this initiative, students need guidance and direction. Effective teaching requires that the teacher suggest concrete topics and activities.

What does the adolescent seek in religion class activities? First, as in many other respects, he needs an outlet for surplus energy. He is anxious to test his newly developed faculties and to find himself. The adolescent shapes his personality largely through activity. His drive for action, however, while a major factor in adolescent psychology, also stems for the dynamic character of the message that challenges him. The child is not satisfied with simply being told the Good News; he wishes to experience it for himself. Through activities the child expresses his faith in a personal and original way. No one else can do this for him. The Word of God is a challenge, a call to the preadolescent, as it is to all people, and requires a response. The student must answer with faith to the revelation presented to him. His activity in religion class becomes an expression of his faith through his own distinctive natural talents and faculties. Such activity both expresses and serves his faith.

The catechist helps the child progress beyond projects which can only be of superficial interest (looking things up, clipping pictures and news items, making posters and mobiles) to those that more permanently and substantially affect the faith-response of the student. The catechist helps the student to give a Christian dimension to his activity and involvement.

Indeed, the catechist attempts to foresee the ultimate aim of such activities. The act of faith elicited during religion class ought not to be limited to the passing moment; it ought not to be a classroom exercise completed at some given time; it ought to be prolonged during the whole life of the student. Eventually the student is to proclaim the Gospel in which he is caught up. Active class participation by adolescents must attain that level if it is to be of true and lasting value. In this way they come to realize that the act of faith constitutes a condition that reaches into every aspect of human behavior.

C. Adolescents want to form a unified group. Adolescents freely and pointedly express the desirability of fellowship among members of a religion class: "We must love one another; we must form a team."—"There should be a warm, brotherly spirit among us."—So in addition to discipline and activity, they want friendship, brotherhood. They want to express themselves, as some twelve-year-olds put it, "as in a family"; they want "to be good friends," "to pray for one another."

Among various suggestions made by preadolescents, one major distinction may be made. Some of their ideas correspond to their stable interests as a group. Other ideas manifest new interests proper to adolescence and a need for interpersonal relationships. The desire for friendship and brotherhood is among these latter.

Why do adolescents attach so much importance to brotherly love and friendship? The need for understanding is profound in adolescents, especially girls. Fulfillment of this need is, therefore, an indispensable condition for a fruitful religion class. The young are very sensitive to the values of friendliness, openness to others, love, sympathy, protection. Sensitive as they are to individual needs and situations, they seek the intimacy of close interpersonal relationship; they develop only in a climate of warm understanding in which they can test their ability to form close relationships. Their receptivity to the living God and their response to Him will be conditioned by their response to others. They make the apprenticeship of their relations with God through the experiences of dealing with their neighbor. It may sometimes happen that the friendship of a classmate or of a grownup is more decisive for the adolescent than membership in a tightly knit group. The group, however, remains very important in his progress towards God. On the other hand, the adolescent finds it extremely difficult to encounter God in an atmosphere in which discord and jealousy are rife. Psychologically, this kind of atmosphere forces him in upon himself, and consequently he is incapable of opening up to Christ, who speaks to him and asks his love.

To realize authentic charity, the preadolescent has to go beyond introspective morality. He must taste the experience of self-giving in order to ascend to the love of Christ. "The surest road to Christ is that of love. One cannot know Christ except in love."—"God is love."

In the eyes of many adolescents, unity within the group is very important, although boys are less sensitive in this regard. Boys need a certain cohesion for working together rather than a close relationship among members of a group. Whereas boys seek unity in action, girls seek rather affective unity. Children often come to religion class in natural groups of two or three. "We go to confession in gangs," a public school student remarked. In view of this phenomenon, the teacher would be ill-advised to break up natural groups of two or three, but he must see to it that these groups do not harm the general class spirit. It is under cordial conditions that the adolescent can give a Christian perspective to his activities and grow in happiness.

D. Adolescents want a religious atmosphere. Adolescents expect the religion class to be different from other classes. "It should not be like other subjects; we have to share in it." What underlies this expectation for an approach different from the usual classroom course? Somehow children realize that religious instruction must touch their whole life. They perceive that it is to affect them vitally and deeply.

The emerging adolescent discovers and encounters perspectives and horizons the existence of which he has never suspected. He seeks a simple and fundamental meaning to his new, bewildering experiences. Unconsciously, he senses that the religion lesson will enlighten and give meaning to the new world he is entering and before which he is dismayed, but in which he must live. Just as in other respects his experience of life is deeper and richer, so, too, the adolescent wishes to bring God into his life in a manner which is more meaningful.

The religion course is an answer to youth's thirst for God. "The class should be more religious," says one adolescent. The teacher has to take this basic need into account. On occasion he should not hesitate to challenge the normal level of comprehension in order that the students may come to realize the complexity and mystery of the divine reality. Students often appreciate such invitations to penetrate more profoundly. In practice, as we will see, certain material conditions will promote a religious atmosphere. However, external conditions are but a means, and the child well knows that the essential prerequisite for religious atmosphere must come from himself. "We must be silent in order to think of God," a teen-ager observes.

II. Organization of the Religion Class

1. Setting the Tone

Adolescents consider that the environment or setting of a religion class is an important factor in its success. In one inquiry 16.5 per cent of the young people questioned cited this factor as essential. Creating a suitable environment makes surrounding circumstances, material or spiritual, conducive to work, prayer, study, or recreation. Students are eager for an atmosphere which will support and help them. What environment do adolescents more or less consciously require?

Setting, or environment, depends on many conditions, some of which are purely material. However, in creating the right climate, the teacher always preserves a spiritual orientation; it is not a matter of producing "conditioned reflexes," of "determining" the young. The teacher's action is primarily concerned with promoting a personal encounter with Christ, the Incarnate Word of God, who reveals Himself in a human, material context.

EXTERIOR SETTING. Students generally are aware of the importance of setting. A lesson that is "different" requires a setting that is "different." One thirteen-year-old suggests using a room near the church or the school chapel. At the very least, the religion classroom should have a special style. A science laboratory derives its proper character from the curious and complex equipment that crowds the room. A history room is lined with volumes that bear witness to the achievements of the past. The religion room creates a sense of the sacred, of mystery, of the divine involvement in the lives of men. A room tastefully decorated with Christian art, which is an expression of man's involvement with God, helps to create a religious atmosphere. During His mortal life, Christ was not indifferent to the setting. He chose a mountain or a lake for certain proclamations. He chose a well to create in the Samaritan woman a thirst for living water. Even in the Old Testament, God revealed Himself in the majestic setting of the desert and of Mount Sinai. So, too, the proper classroom setting provides the teacher with a psychological advantage.

What setting should we prepare for catechesis? It is certainly impossible to change the setting continually, but the aim should be to provide pleasant and agreeable surroundings. A bright, comfortable, attractive room is essential. The usual classroom arrangement of desks should be avoided. As much as possible, adolescents should be allowed to arrange the room themselves, grouping themselves into teams, for example. It would even be advantageous for adolescents to have their own team meeting-place. However, the groups should center around the catechist and not be scattered on all sides.

The furniture should be movable and solid, neither gaudy nor garish. Religious pictures and statues should be in good taste, inspiring prayerfulness, and free of religiosity. They should be changed according to the topics being studied and the liturgical seasons. If finances permit, the room should be set up with adequate audiovisual materials and equipment so that the students may benefit from these valuable educational aids. Adolescents feel all the more at home if they share in decorating the room.

Psychologically, the surroundings of the religion class should satisfy the adolescent's zest for novelty as well as his need for security—he wants to feel at home. Spiritually, they should lead to interior silence and facilitate the opening of the student to God.

ATTITUDE OF THE CATECHIST. The adolescent's emotional life is subject to the many demands of his increasing social involvement. The mounting pressure of marks, of studies, of school schedules, of home problems, and of transportation difficulties brings many tensions and anxieties into the life of a boy or a girl. The student needs, more than ever, to find in the religious instruction class someone who has time to receive him personally, someone who inspires security, someone who allows him to breathe freely, someone whose calm attitude and availability give him interior freedom.

Adolescents are intuitively sensitive to the least sign of sympathy. Subtly, often unconsciously, they evaluate the spirit and personality of the catechist and respond spontaneously; the atmosphere is strained when the catechist is nervous, vague, insecure. Before meeting the class, he should relax and find interior peace. Spiritually, the catechist should become open to the message he is to communicate; he should rededicate himself to his mission in the Church, and enter into a state of communion with others in Christ.

OPENNESS. Anonymity has quickly become one of the marks of our complex modern society. It is not surprising then that the adolescent sometimes feels that he is only a number in the class (Grade 9, No. 1, 2, 3 . . .). During the religious instruction class, he should be allowed to express his individuality and become aware of his own personal value. He should feel that he is *someone* of worth; otherwise he may never be brought to a true encounter with a Person. The catechist, acting in the name of the Church, becomes the catalyst for this encounter. He, therefore, bestows personal attention on each of his pupils. This he may do sometimes by a mere word, a look, and, above all, by use of the Christian name. Such personal contact is essential. Whether or not a girl sustains interest in religion class often depends upon her first encounter with the catechist.

However, in being open with the children, the teacher avoids asking questions which are too personal, too private, too pointed.

Most families are directly or indirectly affected by a variety of delicate situations to which the children are particularly sensitive. Unless such problems are brought up privately by the student, the teacher should make every effort while conducting classroom discussions to respect the family's right to privacy. Probing questions may cause some children to withdraw within themselves because they are loath to reveal their real selves before everyone in the class. Note also that the adolescent becomes aware of himself within the groups of which he forms a part, through the activities in which these groups take part. Frequently, it may be a passing remark which establishes the first favorable contact: the catechist's admiration of a student's art work, or his interest in the children's sports, games, or results in school work. But, at any cost, avoid all the savors of indiscreet probing into personal or family matters.

STARTING POINT. After the welcome, when each child has found his place, the teacher must make a definite break with everything which preceded the lesson. A period of silence, a moment of recollection, of placing oneself in the presence of God, creates an atmosphere of seriousness and evokes concentration. This moment is indispensable to the interiorization of the preadolescent's faith.

The catechist might sometimes ask one of the children to recite a prayer of his own composed during the preceding religion period. If the teacher knows how to make good use of the occasion, he may in this way connect the preceding lesson with the new one. A word or two will recall the discovery made during the preceding class and give definite direction to the present lesson. These few words can whet the appetite of the students for new discoveries.

A recording may be useful as a starting point for a class. Folk music often has lyrics of considerable depth and religious significance. The poetic content is appealing to the young because it is moving and current. Many love songs express an unsatisfied longing. The catechist may attempt to sharpen this sense of discontent and show that it frequently results from lack of spiritual depth in life and love. This discontent, this dissatisfaction may be transformed into the thirst for "living water" which Christ led the Samaritan woman to experience. These and other similar approaches serve to establish the relevance of the good news to the present day and its character of newness.

2. Catechetical Discussion with Adolescents.

Discussion of religion in adolescent classes to be fruitful should have two qualities: (1) it should be conducted with authority and (2) it should be interesting.

AUTHORITY. Adolescents, as previously noted, hold to a degree of discipline in class. The catechist, furthermore, gives a religious character to his class as a necessary condition for the reception of the Word of God. The tone of authority in classroom discussion is of another order, however. It concerns the very manner in which the Word is announced. Because he speaks in the name of the Father in union with Christ and through the Holy Spirit, the catechist acts as "one having authority;" he appeals, he affirms. In him, it is the Church who challenges, who teaches. He has a mandate from the Church of which he must be conscious. The adolescent attains to the transcendence of the absolute God through the catechist acting as a representative of the Church.

To be faithful to the mission he has received from the Church, the catechist should be forewarned against the natural tendency to command according to human standards. He should guard against the subtle psychological danger of desiring to dominate his students and impose self upon them. And, again, he should be aware of the tendency to a pharisaical type of authority, remembering what Christ says of those doctors who used the prestige of their office to impose upon men their own opinions.

Another type of false authority is that which relies solely upon human knowledge. The catechist may be tempted to present a construction that is so rationally compelling and so intellectually perfect that apparently no one can escape the force of its truth. The young bristle instinctively against this type of presentation. They are loath to join in discussion that is led by a teacher who is too overpowering since there is no point in holding discussion with him. Whatever they might say, the catechist always has the last word. While avoiding this attitude, the catechist balances these considerations with the fact that young people respect and want competence. They frequently ask "Why?" In discussing their questions, the catechist has no substitute for preparation, control of material, and total competence in the catechetical situation. Thus, the catechist always remains himself a student.

The ideal authority in class discussion is that of Jesus, whose contemporaries said about him that He spoke "as one having authority" (Mark 1:22). This ideal consists in presenting religion, not as an idea to be discussed, but as a *Person* to be accepted or rejected. Christ asserts, "I am the Truth." There simply is no room for discussion here in the purely rational sense of the word. The catechist should certainly, with deep humility, *speak and declare himself as being Christ in his Church*, with all His weight of Absolute, of Happiness, and of Truth. In this way, he addresses himself to the whole being of youth—to heart, intelligence, and will. He invites the student to take a stand before the Person of this Christ who offers Himself to him. Such authority becomes a call to faith and to an attitude of reverence and respect. The catechist's authority will give place to an easier, more relaxed attitude when the time comes for a more intellectual, more abstract explanation. For adolescents the catechist's bearing and tone of voice should express the reverence and the interior conviction which animate him.

Tone of voice and gestures play a significant part in authoritative teaching. Do not speak too loudly. A low tone maintains calm and allows for accentuating shades of meaning. Intonation should be varied, words well articulated, speech not too rapid, and sentences clear and well constructed. Rhythm of speech should be deliberate and interspersed with silences, since we are dealing with Mystery. The young student should, in fact, sense that he is entering into a reality which arouses admiration and demands clear expression. The secret of the kingdom is not communicated in clamor and shouting; it is passed on as one intimates confidences—reverently, calmly, authoritatively.

On the other hand, in discussing material which involves little of the element of mystery (for example, in presenting the historical fact of the Israelites' crossing the Sea of Reeds), the catechist speaks objectively and factually. Whatever the topic under discussion, he avoids all that seems artificial and tends to cater to natural and sentimental religiosity. He also avoids undue excitement, exaggerated gestures, mimicry, and slang expressions, all of which might distract the attention of the students and invite ridicule. Such excesses could lead to loss of control of the class. Finally, the catechist can realize the proper attitude of authority in discussion if he himself enters completely into the Mystery and is capable of leading his students to share the experience.

INTERESTING DISCUSSION. The presentation of the Christian message should never be boring; it should come through clearly to the students, but it should be interesting. It should be proclaimed precisely as good news. The adolescent who complacently considers himself satisfied with what he has learned in the early grades should get the impression of discovering something new. Young people are quite anxious to be free from those things which are associated with childhood. Such will not be the case unless the message appeals to them freshly as a source of happiness and of life.

In striving for authority and interest in discussion, the teacher faces an extraordinary challenge. He has to be realistic and accept his limitations. He would be deceiving himself if he thinks his students are going to cling to every word. He also has to keep in mind that the religious interests of one group are not the same in every respect as those of another group.

Furthermore, to arouse and sustain student interest at this age, the teacher has to keep in mind certain standards considered important by adolescents themselves. Foremost among these are (1) the relatively important role of sound pedagogical procedure, (2) the importance of presenting religious truths in terms of concrete reality, (3) the need for a central theme, and (4) the need for expression and exchange of ideas.

3. Plan, Unity, and Dialogue. In addition to endowing the catechesis with authority and interest, the religion teacher should emphasize the necessity of (1) a carefully planned, systematically arranged curriculum of religious education, (2) a unfied course in which part is related to part, and all parts to the central whole, and (3) the establishment of dialogue with the adolescent.

PLAN. It is true that adolescents do not want their religion course to be just another subject in the school program. They do expect, however, that the catechist show competence in planning and presenting his course. They want discipline; they want lessons well taught; they want assignments given and evaluated. These expectations show that they are serious about their work. They also wish to gain a certain intellectual satisfaction from it. They want the catechist to respond to their desire for knowledge and understanding of their faith. The catechist cannot disregard these expectations.

The catechist should realize, moreover, that adolescent psychology precludes conversational discussion that is too informal and familiar. Such discussion involves the child too directly without sufficiently respecting his liberty and allowing the saving leeway which allows him to react with freedom. Only serious discussion and firm discipline guarantee that objectivity and purity characteristic of Christ's teaching. It is He, the Word Incarnate, who speaks, and it is He who evokes a response. The very reverence due to the Word of God requires a planned, systematic arrangement of the matter of the religious program. An unstructured religion course presented in a haphazard manner does not command the respect and interest of the students.

On the other hand, without neglecting plan and system, it is necessary to offer the adolescent a message which is close to life and to present it in a very concrete style. This will be done quite naturally if the catechist undertakes to rediscover the message in its pristine form. "There is a great advantage in realizing that Revelation was originally addressed to us, not under the form of abstract propositions, but very concretely as Salvation History. The teaching of religion will not come alive unless we return to the original manifestation of Revelation, unless the Bible, the liturgy, and Salvation History constitute the starting point and the source of all our teaching of dogmatic and moral theology." (Joseph Jungmann, s.j.)

Catechetical discussion, therefore, should be carried on in everyday language. It should make use of stories, examples, comparisons, and personal experiences so as to present a living synthesis. The catechist should not forget that he is reliving, in the presence of and in union with his adolescent pupils, the discovery of God made by this or that biblical personage. His behavior should manifest the here-and-now actuality of God and of the risen Christ. Salvation history is the record of God's involvement in the lives of men. God entered into personal relationships with individuals. The student has to be shown that the experience of Abraham, Moses, Isaac, or David can be his own personal experience through Christ in His Church.

UNITY. The adolescent craves unity. What better unity can we offer him than that of God's revelation of Himself? To it he will himself be progressively led by his personal response of faith, directed towards a more complete commitment to Christ in His Church.

Discussions should not, therefore, be isolated; each one should be seen as a part of the entire catechetical perspective. This unity, it is true, may not be evident at first sight. Given the instability of the adolescent, the religious program can scarcely be linear, and it will frequently be necessary to vary the starting point and the line of development.

The catechist, however, should never lose sight of the purpose to be attained: the proclamation of salvation. He will try to achieve a definite convergence in all his teaching, even while following the adolescent in the meandering ways of his personal search, punctuated as it is by the events of his life. This demands great attention and ability to seize every opportunity for group reflection on the lesson at hand and to teach the child to give a Christian response. The catechist should not improvise according to the whim of the moment or to the prevailing atmosphere. As far as he himself is concerned, he should link up each lesson with the preceding one, without necessarily making the transitional relationship too obvious to the class.

The religion class should not only converge towards a single instructional goal; it should lead the adolescent to unify his life. In fact, during adolescence, the student will actually experience the acute, interior incoherence created by the diversity of the situations in which he finds himself. He will then have the tendency to divide his life into compartments. Religion must not become a mere section of his life, a section which moreover will soon lose its attraction, and which he will be tempted to regard with indifference after receiving the sacrament of Confirmation or after his graduation from school. He must be shown that **God** expects a response from him, one which will take various forms while remaining fundamentally the same, according to the circumstances in which he lives. He will then build up that interior unity in faith and friendship with Christ which will endow him with stability.

DIALOGUE. There must be dialogue between the catechist and the adolescent. Teaching which aims at keeping contact with life must not be purely "occasional;" that is to say, it must not be given only as an opportune occasion arises, for it would not only betray the message itself, but would also neglect a whole area of adolescent life. In a group lesson, the teacher risks missing many of the reactions and questions of the individual student. Moreover, each student, being a person, has his own particular pattern of life, his own personal moments of crisis and synthesis which do not necessarily correspond with those of his neighbor. This is why the catechist should contact his students personally outside of class; he can later adapt his course to answer questions which, if left unasked, would puzzle adolescents all their lives. The core of the lesson, however, must be a dialogue either following the discussion or during some activity (question-and-answer period, group research) to which the catechist contributes examples from his own daily experience and in which he is open to the contributions of his pupils and their viewpoints.

4. Discussion Based on a Theme

A. What is a catechetical theme? The theme is the single general idea which expresses with the greatest fidelity what God says to man in the course of a particular event in salvation history. It is an idea which dynamically directs the unfolding of the discussion and of the whole lesson. To express it more precisely, the theme is a universal proposition underlying an entire lesson and expressing a doctrinal reality in such a way that it both reaches the deepest interests of the group and at the same time arouses and provides a focus for the thought and action of the group.

It expresses a relationship. The theme expresses a God-man relationship since it stands precisely at the meeting-point of the human situation and the Word of God. It is not an abstract proposition, a pure idea. It does not consist, for example, in the theoretical study of one's vocation to be faithful to God. It would be expressed thus: God calls man to a life more beautiful and higher than the one which man of himself expects.

It is true to the objectivity of the message. The theme is true to the Word which is objectively contained in an event, a text, or a dogmatic definition. For example, the revelation given on Mount Sinai is not primarily that of the holiness of God before a sinner, as is the case in the theophany of Isaia, but a revelation of God's loving choice of a people to be His own.

It has immediacy. The catechetical theme expresses a general idea capable of speaking to man today, especially the young people to whom it is addressed in the classroom. For example, through Abraham, God calls man through faith to the promised land. Here especially, the theme expresses the Word of God with maximum immediacy for the young today. For example, to a group of boys who have been placed in a tiresome religious climate, the teacher announces the theme of Abraham: "When God calls man, He always calls him to the happiness of a promised land". The teacher can never overlook this most essential quality of a catechetical theme. It is his most important responsibility. It is his task to be aware of the immediacy of the message and to communicate its immediacy to the young who expect it. To do this the teacher must know the world of the adolescent, his magazines, friends, social behavior, TV programs, and so forth.

B. Preparation of discussion based on a theme. In preparing a catechetical discussion for adolescents, the catechist (1) chooses the theme and (2) determines which event, parable, story, or deed will provide the best framework for the lesson.

Choosing the Theme. It is frequently difficult to discover the theme, to find a single idea around which all points of discussion will crystalize, which will give dynamic unity to the exposition, and which will elicit definite spiritual attitudes. Some teachers seem to come almost intuitively upon theme and illustrative facts and examples; others require intensive reflection and extensive research. The following analysis may aid both types of teachers in choosing the theme.

1. **Try to see things with the perspective of the adolescent by systematic study and by sympathetic attitude.** Adolescents, distressed by the impact of new experiences, want their religion teacher to be someone who "is with it," who is understanding. The teacher will never reach the adolescent in any significant degree unless he resorts to the adolescent's frame of reference, unless he shares his experiences. How does the teacher arrive at this? Without doubt, temperament plays a great role here. But there is more: the Christian educator seeks to share the sentiments of these young people in order to be one of them. Because of his union in Christ, he is urged on by the Lord's infinite charity to seek to become "all things to all men."

The teacher uses a variety of approaches to assure response from his students. He may, for instance, casually sound out their opinions on topics to be studied. "What does God mean to you?"— "Are there any topics which you would like to have discussed in religion class?"—"What do your friends think of religion, of God?" This simple approach gives anonymity to opinions expressed. In making it seem that the teacher is asking assistance from the students, it brings him closer to them.

Again, the teacher takes into account the family life of his students and the neighborhood in which they live. "As far as I am concerned," one priest remarked, "it is thanks to contacts with families that I have been able to emerge from the abstract world in which I had been living."

Some understanding of current "teen culture" is indispensable. The teacher must be aware of adolescent interests and activities, many of which are reflected in the mass media. The teacher has to know what his students talk about, what sports they enjoy, what books and magazines they read. Periodicals like *Time*, *Newsweek*, and *Look* publish valuable studies of various aspects of "teen culture." The teacher should consider time and effort in exploring the teen world as an integral part of his in-service training and education.

South Pacific is a film known to teacher and students alike. It reflects student ways of thinking, seeing, and feeling. It belongs to teen culture. Now suppose the catechist is preparing to speak to his class of the kingdom of heaven. Viewed in Christian perspective, *South Pacific* calls to mind the need of the human heart with regard to the kingdom which the catechist is to announce. It may be considered a timely, modern parallel of a lost paradise. It can serve to introduce the theme of the kingdom of heaven. "The kingdom of God is like an island in the South Pacific."

Splendor of sunsets and idealized colors in the film strike the young at the sense level. Penetrating stereophonic music evokes the notion of omnipresence. The spirit of pageant and dance is an invitation to the plenitude which the *Exultet* also seeks to express. Universal love, personal friendship, idealization of woman, interracial brotherhood — all these inundate the young through a flood of sensible forms. In one respect, *South Pacific* is a story form similar to that of the parable of the wedding garment. All these aspects of the film can serve the catechist in presenting the theme of the kingdom of heaven.

In presenting the message of the Bible, of the prophets, of Jesus, the catechist speaks in contemporary idiom in order to bring the good news close to the heart of his audience. He makes Isaia come to life; he makes the prophet's experience a meaningful reality in Christian living today. This is indispensable to the relevance of Isaia here and now. The catechist is careful, however, not to lead the students to misunderstand the nature of the kingdom. The kingdom of God is not a natural phenomenon; it is God living and acting within us. A good catechist does more than observe people's reactions and read *Life* magazine. He sees all human realities in their relationship to the kingdom of God.

The catechist who teaches adolescents perceives the interplay of the human and the divine. He speaks of the Christian Mystery in terms of human experience. He projects on man's least action or aspiration the light of God, who comes to fulfill and save man. Such was the catechesis of the prophets, of Jesus, of the Fathers of the Church. Jesus' words, "I am the bread of life," presuppose that He is familiar with human hunger and seeks to relieve it. He sincerely sympathizes with the hungry. But what is infinitely more, the words of Christ presuppose that He projects into man's hunger His true knowledge of man. Jesus knows what human flesh and blood do not know. He realizes profundly that the deepest hunger of man is hunger for the kingdom of God, and because

He knows it, He says, "I am the true bread."

The catechist places these words of Jesus in the context of the modern world. When asked what is the most important problem to be solved in the next twenty years, a group of heads of states recently answered: "It is the problem of hunger in the world. It is intolerable that two thirds of humanity should be dying of hunger while the other third have more than enough to eat." The catechist subscribes to this declaration, but going further and deeper, he asserts that the most urgent problem in the world is that of the spiritually underfed. He shows pictures and cites articles from newspapers and magazines as heartrending evidence that countless people in the world are dying of starvation. He also produces even more tragic evidence that countless people in the world have been unable to establish the kingdom of God, the kingdom of peace and love through, with, and in Jesus Christ. He asserts that it is intolerable that three quarters of all mankind know nothing of the Eucharist, which is the sacramental expression of love among members of the kingdom.

What the catechist needs, therefore, is a deep sense of the divine-human encounter. He has to sharpen his belief in prayer and in spiritual fellowship. To announce God in biblical style is to link heaven with earth. The catechist gives to human experience a divine dimension. The permanent, sensible, visible link between God and man today is the Church, it is we speaking in the Church. It is through us, the Church, that the biblical word is transmitted in its sacramental vigor, that is to say, sensibly and efficaciously.

2. As an aid in choosing the theme, read the Bible from the viewpoint of an adult Christian, but keep in mind the mentality of the adolescent. The message will strike the catechist in its totality but with a very specific interest in mind. In perusing salvation history, the teacher ought to discern and record certain pertinent words, attitudes, and facts which are particularly suitable for adolescent catechesis; for example, in the story of Moses: "No one can look on God and live."

3. Analyze your emotional reactions to the Word of God. Confronted with the Word of God, the catechist experiences im-

pressions of fright and bewilderment, sentiments of fear, of commitment, of admiration. He then notes which dominant emotional response should emerge during the class discussion.

4. Analyze from a threefold viewpoint the precise relationship which God establishes with you through His Word: What is the objective content of what God says to you? What does He wish to convey to me when, on Mount Sinai, He asserts: "I am the Wholly Other. I am who am"? Look for precise words to express this passage.

In what manner has this Word of God touched me personally? *"Quidquid recipitur ad modum recipientis recipitur."* ("Whatever is received is received according to the mode of the receiver.") Then try to state precisely the particular way in which, linked as you are with the adolescent, you have been affected. Did you identify personally with Moses as he encountered God? Did you become aware of God's transcendence through an objective, rational exposition? Or through an impersonal reading of the text?

What particular aspect of your psychology, of your situation, of your aspirations is affected by the Word of God? On Sinai, for example, your desire to see God, your curiosity and your need for heaven were stirred, evangelized, and corrected.

5. From this threefold viewpoint, establish a synthesis based on the biblical text. Your psychological situation is this: You wish to know, you wish to see God. Your relation with God and His Word consists in your identifying yourself personally with Moses in his encounter with God. The objective Word of God, expressed and seen in the full light of Christ and of His Church, asserts: "I am infinitely near, infinitely involved in man's innermost being, and yet infinitely different from him."

Your synthesis would be this: "I wish to come to some personal understanding of God in the meeting of Moses with God on Mount Sinai... God appears to me quite other than I had imagined Him... infinitely near by His goodness, yet infinitely different from me." Religious experience arises out of prayerful study.

Note. According to the need of certain adolescents, the catechist should insist on certain points which are objectively secondary;

for example, the feeling of bewilderment caused by the encounter with God.

6. Broaden your particular synthesis into a general theme for discussion. The catechist always sees that the general theme retains its role of relating revelation and the good news to the needs of man. For example, when man meets the true God, he discovers the One who transcends him and his ideas. When God utters his real name (when God reveals Himself), man is seized by the extraordinary revelation of the One who by nature is personally inaccessible to man.

7. Arrange the theme in concrete detail. The catechist takes the key points, those words and deeds best adapted to the psychology of adolescents. Starting with these, he reviews the whole procedure and crystalizes the theme. For example, with regard to Moses ascending the mountain, Moses in the crevice of the rock, the catechist emphasizes certain important recorded details, certain phrases, certain images, either in the discussion or in the activities that follow it. But he is careful that nothing distracts the children's attention from the theme.

Determining the Element Which Crystalizes the Theme of the Lesson. The adolescent needs a theme couched in terms of an action or an image which serves as the framework of the lesson upon which the discussion will hinge. To be of value, the action or the image should meet certain requirements. It should be clearly expressive of the intent of God's revelation. This is the objective content of the theme. It should be in keeping with the adolescent's manner of thinking and feeling. Thus, adolescents are more impressed by Moses' hiding in the cleft of the rock than they are by the trumpets and the lightning.

Again, the catechist himself should feel strongly about the theme. In fact, since it is by way of the Word lived and expressed by the catechist that the adolescent receives the message, it would be good for the catechist himself to live intensively the biblical fact which he is discussing. Otherwise, the concrete fact loses its aptness and its weight as a symbol. The catechist himself loses his vital meaning. It is a well-known fact that no one can inspire admiration for something which he himself does not admire. Deception has no place in catechesis. Neither should the catechist impose some point which is of vital interest to himself and yet which may be of little relevance to his students. The theme will be all the closer to biblical pedagogy in the measure in which it leads to greater communication among God, the catechist, and the adolescent.

8. Prayer. The religion lesson is not truly religious unless it leads effectively to an awakening of faith. Faith itself is not truly faith unless it issues forth into an act of personal response to God who has spoken. Speaking *of* God is vacuous if it does not lead to speaking *to* God.

"We ought always to pray," Christ tells us. And pray we must during the course of religious instruction. Prayer will consist then in turning attention towards the God who speaks. There should reign over all catechesis an atmosphere of contemplation so that the "prayer" properly so called will be deeply expressive of communion with God. The moments of prayer must themselves be prepared.

Prayerful Atmosphere. To create a prayerful atmosphere, the teacher asks for silence and correct posture. Posture is especially important for adolescents. The catechist himself sets the atmosphere of prayer by his example. If all during prayer he is continually watching the children, he cannot pray himself, nor can he lead the children to pray.

Intentions. Specifying intentions for which to pray risks awakening merely natural sentiments of pity, joy, or generosity, without training the children to Christ-like prayer. A simple psychological stimulus can very well lead to a kind of natural piety which consists in wishing to obtain certain spiritual effects by the use of human means. The profound significance of intention in prayer is not so much to awaken and to move as to unify the community in charity, to gather all lives into a single sheaf so that they may achieve unity in Christ under the eyes of God. If the teacher aims at this goal, it will be good to have the children themselves suggest the intentions.

Manner of praying. The following suggestions aim to help the adolescent at prayer:

Vary prayer formulas, avoiding those which are habitual and stereotyped in favor of more spontaneous and flexible ones.

Choose the short prayer, generally taken from the missal: a passage from a psalm, a hymn, a refrain. Young people themselves usually prefer "a short prayer which says something."

Lead the adolescent gradually to pray alone, in the presence of God. He should progressively experience that prayer is not always saying something but rather turning towards God, listening to God.

Occasionally ask the children to pray as they listen to the reading of a Bible passage, while they are attending to the Word of God.

After a discussion, have a group compose and write a prayer on the chalkboard while the rest of the class engages in some other activity.

Have each student in turn prepare a prayer.

Make up prayer cards from which the students may choose their own prayers.

Now and then post on the bulletin board a copy of a prayer composed by a student.

Write the words of a new prayer on the chalkboard. Summarize the central thought or sentiment of the prayer, and give the children time to familiarize themselves with the thought and the words of the prayer.

Encourage the students to imagine the disposition with which biblical personages prayed: David reciting the Miserere, Mary proclaiming the Magnificat.

Express the lesson topic in a prayer, making it a stepping-stone to God.

Assign the writing of a prayer as an activity in the lesson. Use the prayer as a transition by reciting it at the beginning of the next lesson.

It is important that the prayer not be an artificial formality but rather a spontaneous expression of the religious sentiments of a community of youngsters.

The timing of prayer is most important. Usually it should be suggested at the climax of discussion. However, there need not be explicit prayer at each session. An excellent prayer consists in allowing for activity which will foster assimilation and meditation on what has been discussed. If certain pupils are unwilling to pray, they must be left free, so long as they cause no disturbance. The catechist should take precaution lest, at this time of life when a spirit of independence awakens in youth, prayer appear as a constraining burden. The catechist ought not to be indiscreet in imposing formulas, reflections, and resolutions which are too personal.

9. Activities. Three types of catechetical activities may be distinguished: preparatory activities, activities within the lesson, and assimilative activities.

Preparatory Activities. The goal of preparatory activities is to dispose the group to receive the Word of God. This type of activity leads the students to pose a single basic question and to seek an answer to it with interest and anticipation. Precatechetical activities create the proper atmosphere and center attention on the principal theme of the lesson. They may consist of playing a recording, writing a meaningful sentence on the chalkboard, displaying a picture from a magazine, reading an item fom a newspaper. The activity pinpoints the question to which the lesson will give the answer.

A widely used form of preparation activity is that of the questionnaire. The catechist must, however, be on guard against going to extremes with adolescents in this respect. Their personal experience is still too restricted to allow of many real problems. The questions asked often seem to them artificial, too objective, and too irrelevant to their lives. At this stage, other methods which are more probing and concrete seem preferable. Instead of starting off with questions aimed at the adolescent's subjectivity, the catechist starts off with facts, sayings, pictures, showing situations which of themselves spark questions. One procedure is strongly recommended for use with young people. The group is divided into subgroups of six or seven, each having a leader. Each subgroup is given a picture (for example, a news photo) with two or three questions to be answered.

Activities within the Lesson. This very special type of activity has for its aim not so much to have the group assimilate, as to have them express the wealth of knowledge and a Christian living they more or less implicitly possess. In one sense, this activity replaces the lesson. It presupposes that the members of the group already have some doctrinal knowledge.

The teacher can stimulate research by raising real questions, elicit self-expression on the part of those having more knowledge or experience, and have the group progress on that basis. Undoubtedly when working along such lines, the catechist must feel free to conclude the discussion with a more explicit exposition of the issue at hand, or with a clear and precise summary. But the essential point remains the effort at common research and the pooling of the resources of the class.

With regard to this technique, two items are to be noted:

1. The technique of group discussion cannot be improvised. It presupposes on the part of the leader real competence, that is to say, knowledge of the dynamics of group discussion, presence to the group and ability to relate religious doctrine with the reactions of young people, and mastery of the question at issue.

2. Group discussion also supposes a certain quality in the group itself, a quality characterized by freedom to ask questions, to express oneself, and to listen.

The latter condition causes leaders to believe that this type of procedure is to be more advantageously used at the older adolescent level.

Nevertheless, so important is this technique to accustom the young to express themselves and to communicate on the spiritual plane that it seems indispensable, even at the very beginning of preadolescence. It can be done only with the help of very specific rules and the strict observance of such rules.

Assimilative Activities. These techniques are better known and are being currently used at the catechetical level. They aim not only at an intellectual assimilation of the message, but at fostering a personal response in faith. Let us mention only notebooks, panel or round-table discussions, scrapbooks, reports of research, and use of audiovisual aids.

It is important to note concerning collective activities that in spite of their attractiveness, they risk being superficial, if they are not the fruit of personal effort. The catechist might sometimes use, especially when the children are tired, activities which are more relaxing: interviews, individual and group inquiries, and the like. To avoid the diffusion of the student's attention, prepare questionnaires based on essentials.

II. Teaching Salvation History to Adolescents

I To What Extent Salvation History Is Catechesis

1. Introduction

A. Young people prefer facts to theory.

They reject as too abstract a catechesis based exclusively on a study of the nature of things. Abstractions do not appeal to twentieth-century man.

The enthusiasm excited among young people by the writings of Teilhard de Chardin attests to their love of the concrete. Father Teilhard's thought is nourished by experimental science; it is close to facts, to life. Not unlike the great St. Thomas, who sought to reconcile Christian revelation and the philosophy of the Greeks, Teilhard de Chardin initiated a dialogue between faith and the experimental sciences. In the twentieth century, practically all of human endeavor confines itself almost exclusively to the realms of science and technology. Youth are very much a part of the technological age. They have a mentality which provides striking contrast to that of two or three generations ago. Teilhard presents concepts and challenges which are particularly meaningful and exciting to the youth of today.

B. Young people do not fully grasp the present-day relevance of past events.

Historical events are too often presented without reference to their actual meaning. Teachers often fail to derive from them principles of thought and laws of action applicable to the present and the future. A militant Marxist voiced the following opinion when speaking to a Christian: "Your Christ is a risen Christ . . . What do I care? The only question which interests me is, what is He doing today?"

The catechist in high school often has to adjust himself to the fact that his student has received many of the biblical events in grade school as stories. It is his rather difficult task to present these same stories with new depth, with new dimension, with relevance to the vital situation of teen-agers.

C. Young people are interested in the future.

Certainly, there is no question here of a general and theoretical systematization of the sense of history, but rather of a certain feeling of the growth of the world with which the lot of these young people is linked. "The favorite theme of the young is not history but self-fulfillment, happiness, success, efficiency." (J. Folliet) But this uneasiness regarding self-fulfillment and the search for the laws of success quickly dovetail into a more global preoccupation about the future of man. With its particular forward-looking way of appraising facts, events, and things, by the uneasiness and excitement which it arouses as to the possible future of man, our era fosters in young people openmindedness to this sense of history. Hence the importance of salvation history in catechesis. Biblical acts have religious meaning. They manifest the intervention of a God who actuates man's becoming. Thus, these acts call for decision—the making of the future. The adolescent's interest is aroused if he sees that these acts are of importance in his own personal development. They provide an excellent springboard for the adolescent's reflections.

2. **Christian Concept of the Study of History.** *Starting Point.* As in all study of history, the Christian must begin by studying observable facts through marks left in the world. However, the facts of biblical history, as against those of scientific history, are not simply natural; they are divine events culminating in the resurrection and the Church. God reveals Himself in these events; in them, man glimpses God's "behavior and thought."

Historical Systematization. According to present day historical philosophies, Marxism among others, history does not consist in a simple determination of facts, or even in the determination of constants. The Christian must establish the "historical sense" on a higher level, that is to say, its orientation and its motion. Today and tomorrow must be enlightened by yesterday.

In an analogous manner, but on a higher level, the Christian sense of history, with all it entails, flows from a permanence of meaning and of direction in a series of events. It is not a question, for example, of wishing to deduce Christian teaching from a single fact, for instance that of the call of Abraham, or even from an essential but isolated event, such as the resurrection. The crucial event which is the resurrection must be appraised in its context:

ABRAHAM—the father of the chosen people setting out towards the land of Canaan.

THE EXODUS—the chosen people marching towards the Promised Land.

THE LIBERATION FROM EXILE—the small remnant of the chosen people clustering around God's Temple.

THE RESURRECTION—the birth of the Church and entry into the New Earth.

It is the risen Christ who injects meaning into all historical events, and hence into all human values and aspirations. The nation of the baptized marching with the risen Christ towards the New Earth was prefigured by the clan of Abraham trekking towards Canaan under God's orders. Discovering the Christian sense of history consists, then, in linking together those events which reveal God's ways and disclose His presence. From these events, the Christian is enlightened *about God and His works, about the meaning of man of the present and future.*

In common with other philosophies of history, salvation history interprets observable facts. There is, however, an essential difference: the interpretation of biblical facts is a matter of faith. It consists in discerning the supernatural character of the events, and it issues in acceptance of supernatural revelation, that is, the sublime thought and action of God, the guide of history revealed in the events. Such an outlook presages what the catechesis should be, not an accumulation of facts, nor a juxtaposition of historical events, but a revelation of God made flesh in human history.

3. The Facts on Which the Christian Sense of History Rests.

A. *When may an event be called "divine?"* An event is called "divine" when God intervenes in it and commits Himself. A divine

C

act or deed is one revealing a dialogue between God and man which reveals a *covenant.*[1]

B. *What are the divine events?*

THE GREAT DIVINE EVENT. The great divine event, the permanent, observable fact in which God reveals Himself today in act, is *His Church*—the social sacrament which bears witness to the saving involvement of God in the lives of men: "A sign raised among the nations." Such is the essential event, bearer of Revelation, the global fact on which the Christian faith focuses. There can, therefore, be no catechesis unless this *here-and-now* fact be first manifested. To the statement, "Jesus Christ is ineffectual," the first answer, even before that of the resurrection, is "the scandal of the Church."

THE OTHER DIVINE DEEDS. In this Church—in its memory, in its consciousness—are present all the historical deeds of its past, deeds which can stand the test of scientific scrutiny by the unbeliever. These deeds are preserved principally in the Bible, considered as salvation history, that is, as the history of the events in which God has intervened historically to speak to man and to save him. These facts are "very certain signs" which guarantee the fact which is the Church and enlighten it.

C. *When is an event a "revealing" event?* Revelation comes into play when naturally observable deeds appear "treated," modified by *forces, intentions,* or *meanings* beyond *natural reason;* for example, the clan of Abraham sets out under an impulse from on high.

It is in this sense that the divine event is radically different from the natural one. It is a natural phenomenon just as is any historical deed. However, it is a phenomenon which reflects "unbelievable" dimensions, which eludes the "natural." Doubtless, this fact does not constrain the mind; otherwise faith would be compulsory. But it is proposed to man as a "disturbing sign," a "call" and also,

---

1 Revelation is relation: God enters into an eternal relationship with historical man to enlighten him and to save him. Revelation begins when the God-man relation begins; it culminates when God becomes incarnate. Revelation, as relation, because it reaches man, becomes salvation history. There is a salvation history event every time there is a God-man encounter.

in the case of a miracle, as "a very certain sign." Faith is discerning the divine modality God gives to natural events, and perceiving the intentions and meanings hidden behind divine events.

4. How Salvation History Is Catechesis. Catechesis is not the transmission of a theory, but of a fact the deeper meaning of which, transmitted and guaranteed by the Church, enlightens, calls, and causes man to be reborn to a new life.

A. Transmission of divine deeds having "supernatural" meaning. History is catechesis inasmuch as it is the transmission of divine facts and of the "supernatural" meaning of these divine facts. The story of Abraham is not in itself catechetical; catechesis comes into play when the fact is transmitted with its supernatural meaning, that is, with interpretations and systematic organization deriving from faith.

FIRST EXAMPLE: Presentation of a divine event with emphasis on significance.

The crossing of the Red Sea. The Church must tell the story as a soldier returning from war tells of his exploits in battle, what he saw, what he did. What must be stressed is the manner in which God waits till the last minute (in order to try one's *faith*) to save his people. Enthusiasm following victory is aroused by the knowledge that it is a gift of the saving God. In order the better to bring this out, the Christian adopts the point of view of the "people" (the Church) who *experience* God. The historical change wrought for the people by the action of God brought their discovery of God. God revealed Himself. (For example, Miriam at the campfire, at night. See below for procedures to be followed.)

SECOND EXAMPLE: Can we give a catechetical presentation of Palestine? How?

Principle. In order that biblical geography be effective catechesis, all geographical places must refer to Jesus Christ. They must be taught in connection with Jesus Christ, as a sign of what He is, of what He loves, of what He thinks and does eternally.

Application. At Bethlehem, Jesus says to the Christian, "This is My background—humble people, simple folk, farming country, piles of stones." It is He who makes the Christian visit Bethlehem, or rather it is the Church which preciously guards the remembrance of His birth as a sign of the kind of man He was. The place, the people to whom He revealed Himself—nothing is irrelevant. All this is the matter, the sign of His intentions. All this is the reality of the Incarnation.

B. Transmission by the Church. There is no catechesis, in the Catholic sense of the word, except when the Biblical events are proclaimed by that *divine, essential, and actual being which is the Church.* In fact, if they are to be catechetical, biblical events must be consistent with the present-day Church and delivered in harmony with it. They must be a part of the life of the Church. God is not bound to the letter of the Bible, but to the Church, which is its Spirit. "I am with *you* all days, even to the end of time," says the Lord. Christ, the historical personage, has become the Ecclesial Christ. We, the people of God, bring Christ to the world. The Church is the actual revelation of Jesus Christ; it is in the Church that the call to Abraham and the invitation to Exodus resound; it is the Church which witnesses the resurrection. It is up to the catechist, witness to the Church, to insist on the mystery of Jesus continued in her.

5. How the Catechesis of Past Events of Salvation History Can Be Made Actual. Catechesis is not truly such unless it is actual, that is to say, unless it concerns the man of today. It is not sufficient to present such or such a person of the past as a model to follow today. ("Do as Jesus did . . . adopt the attitude of faith of Moses as he stood before God . . .") Personages and events must issue a call to man to enter into a dialogue exchanged *in present-day terms.* In fact, the only reason their experiences are recorded is the vital pertinence they have to our own personal life.

CONDITIONS:

a. The biblical fact must be presented by the Church. A biblical fact acquires present-day value inasmuch as it is the Church, calling men to salvation, which proclaims and renews the biblical fact in the life of the Christian community. The catechist should have recourse to the liturgy, which is the realization of the call. Catechesis achieves maximum effectiveness when linked with the sacraments. For example, the Exodus must be discovered in a paschal, baptismal context. The use of holy water becomes a lifelong symbol of it.

b. The biblical fact should be presented in such a way that the divine intention is shown to the student as something which concerns him today. God continues to insert Himself in the Christian community, the Church. A study of the divine encounters of the past enables us to perceive with depth the role of the people of God today.

c. Finally, this deed or fact must be perceived by a person who is subjectively disposed for conversion. A biblical fact will be all the more pertinent for someone who is ready to be converted in depth by responding to the divine action discovered therein. Such a person will seek from this event something more than the revelation of a merely natural significance to human life.

6. How Biblical History Can Lead to Faith. This is the key question which summarizes all the preceding ones: *How does biblical history educate?* Salvation history leads to faith through events, actions, words, and personages wherein God has hidden His Presence and His Actions. To educate by way of salvation history is to put modern man in contact with the eternal thought and action of God as lived in past centuries and relived today by the Church. To educate by way of salvation history is to unlock biblical revelation; that is to say, to show concretely, for the benefit of modern adolescents, how God speaks and how man is challenged. Every hero, every concrete fact is eloquent insofar as it causes this dialogue between God and humanity to burst forth. For example, that God should have spoken to Abraham may leave us cold. But when we become aware that we are Abraham, that God does not change His mind, that the Covenant is eternal, and that God's promises hold good for us, the picture changes totally.

HOW TO GIVE A BIBLICAL CATECHESIS. The whole secret of biblical education consists in having the man of today again contacted, enlightened, and saved by this God who continues to manifest Himself for us in the biblical events. The word uttered historically by Moses must become historically actual to the young people of today. And confronted with this word they must renew the commitment of Moses, of the Apostles, and of all other saints who penetrated into the world of the divine calling. To make *the dialogue between God and man* living and actual for adolescents—this is the crux of biblical education. The students must be shown that the fascination exerted by God on the youthful David can be equally magnetic between God and the young people of today. And the word spoken to David can resound as a very concrete invitation for today's young boy or girl to enter into the holy covenant and confide to the God of life the fulfillment of his existence. But it is the catechist's responsibility to know the world and mentality of his students so that he can present God's invitation which is now very much a part of his own life.

An education which does not enlighten and lead students to the kingdom of God is not a biblical education, but a natural one. Salvation history must not be reduced to a parade of beautiful examples or to a lesson in secular history. When the Fathers of the Church taught religion, the Bible was nothing other than a proclamation of the Church concerning the living God. Biblical deeds were presented in such a way as to involve the listener actively, to enlighten him, and to save him. In much the same way, our students must be brought to realize that salvation history today continues as the life of the Church, which is not something formal or purely functional, but especially since Vatican II, a challenging involvement in the affairs of our technological age. The call of Abraham, Moses, Luke, and Paul is now the call of Bill, Mike, Susan, and Patricia to establish peace, justice, love, in the age of the computer, of nuclear power, and of unparalleled affluence. In the classroom, certain concrete problems of catechesis arise. Which are the divine events on which we should stress most? When teaching the history of the Old Testament, must we continually refer to Jesus Christ?

The following are suggested as possible solutions:

a. No divine event should be interpreted outside the pale of the full light given to us by Jesus Christ, the Divine Event par excellence. When the meaning of a friend's gesture is not clear, we demand more evident signs. Now the evident gesture of God, that which allows of no error, is Easter. Death is the deed which indicates most clearly the direction of a man's life, and the resurrection is the most significant testimony to the power and design of God.

All catechesis, then, should be seen, explained, or expressed in view of the mission of Jesus Christ. When we speak of Abraham, we must show that his faith in the Promised Land finds its fulfillment in Jesus Christ. Jesus realizes within Himself all the words God has addressed to the world. It is in this sense that Christ fulfills the Law and the Prophets. Creation itself lacks meaning except in its reference to Jesus. (See the prologue of the Gospel of St. John, 1:1-4.) Is creation not the beginning of the gathering together of all creatures in Jesus Christ for whom and in whom everything has been made?

The core of all biblical catechesis, therefore, is always Easter, and Easter is itself the pledge of the resurrection of all flesh in Jesus (Parousia).

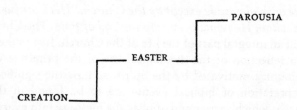

b. The resurrection of Jesus judges the world. There is something *final* about it, and this character of finality reveals the meaning of everything else, including natural creation. The first creation cannot even be understood if we lose sight of the new creation.

However, the connection between a biblical fact and the risen Christ may sometimes be only implicit in catechesis. When the catechist speaks of Abraham, he does not necessarily speak of the Lord. But he does not speak of the father of believers as would Sarah, because, in the light of Jesus' life, he knows the meaning of Abraham's life. In like manner, the catechist understands the full meaning of the Hebrews' deliverance, because Jesus has revealed it by His words and deeds; and it is this understanding alone which gives to the catechist a distinctive quality of precision and light. The Christian educator knows that "Egypt" of the Book of Exodus still exists; as a condition it is our world inasmuch as it is considered to be under the power of Satan. The catechist knows that God really has passed through history to snatch man from the forces of a corrupt and powerless world: Exodus is Easter. He knows that every man is called in the footsteps of Christ to enter into the Promised Land of the resurrection and of the kingdom.

By his word and by bearing witness to his own salvation, the catechist announces by means of the Jewish Pasch that the Pasch of Christ has arrived. With St. Paul he says: "to me, though I am the very least of all the saints, this grace was given, to preach to the Gentiles the unsearchable riches of Christ . . ." (Ephesians 3:8).

   c. *The Christ-Event and all the events, words, and deeds of Christ's life (of nearly 2000 years ago now) cannot be transmitted to me with plenitude except by the Church, "His Faithful Spouse," with whom He remains even to the end of time.* The Christ-Event is still an integral part of the life of the Church. Just as the Gospels are a reflection of the theological life of the primitive Christian community motivated by the Spirit, so now the significance and interpretation of biblical events are to be found in the living Church, which carries and applies the message into every facet of human endeavor. The truth of Jesus Christ is given us by the Church, which explains the true meaning of biblical events.

   Consider this analogy: a great man has just died; someone wants to write his life, to relate the events which marked it. Whom does he consult first and foremost? Naturally, he turns to the man's wife, with whom the man has lived, to whom he confided his secrets, for whom he dies. The writer is not barred from access to others, friends or neighbors; each may have a word or an opinion to add. But the final point of reference is the man's wife.

   The catechist might develop this comparison of a woman's understanding of her husband to bring out the role of the Church. Because she knows how important certain times or certain places were in the life of her husband, a wife will keep mementos, classify them, sort them out, and save the most precious. In like manner, the Church, Spouse of the Lord, keeps the documents which reveal Him (Gospels), stresses essential events, de-emphasizes the merely accessory. The Church alone can assign the proper place and meaning to biblical events.

d. *In what act, at what moment, does the Church best transmit to us the memory of the Lord?* At what moment does she make Him known to us with maximum truth, fidelity, realism, and effectiveness?

One might think that it is when the Church defines a dogma. Yet although dogmatic definitions rigorously outline the content of the "memory" of the Church, it is not through them that we penetrate this memory in a living, active manner. Conciliar definitions are ordained to another end, namely, the encounter of humanity with its Lord. Their purpose is to make the Eucharistic act truer, more faithful and to lead to total communion. Ultimately, the culminating point of the revelation of the Church, the light which radiates through all past events and clarifies them all, is the Eucharist, lived in its liturgical fullness. The Eucharist is salvation history perfectly realized in a sacamental act. It is the sacramental act of a community whose members are related to one another in a bond of love in and through Jesus Christ. What is existing among the members in their own lives is now expressed sacramentally.

Therefore, it may be concluded:

1. The eminent act in which the Church transmits its history is the Eucharist; it is the *memorial* par excellence.

2. All the liturgy hinges on the Eucharistic act. The liturgy is the total act of the sanctified and sanctifying Church.

3. The Church is, then, most the Church in the Eucharistic Celebration.

The liturgical act is that by which the Church evokes for the Christian only the memory of her Lord but renders actually present His deeds and gesture, His eternal action. The liturgy is the Church in the act of recalling Christ, her Lord, who is now forever before the Father and who gives meaning to the world from creation until the end of time. The Bible is the record of God's involvement in the human history of the present. The liturgy is the earthly manifestation of Jesus eternally before His Father. That is why biblical catechesis should be nurtured on a revitalized liturgy.

To establish a program as well as to decide on the best pedagogical methods to use, one must refer first to the type of catechetical procedure proper to the liturgy. This exigency explains the importance given later to the pedagogical procedure of "retrospection." This is the procedure the Church uses when, refusing to adopt a purely chronological perspective of history, she builds up her calendar on the basis of her own understanding of the past.

II Methodology for the Presentation of Salvation History to Adolescents

1. **The Problem.** Once the meaning of the objective events transmitted by the Church (God's intentions) are clear in his mind, how is the catechist going to present the biblical events in catechesis to a particular age group in such a way that they will be as enlightening and enriching as possible to the young? It is a question of discovering the pedagogical guidelines which will be most suitable to the mentality of the young and to the "Memoria" of the Church, that is to say, to Tradition, both as to objective content and as to method.

The teacher will add to these guidelines the information which the friends of Jesus, His kindred, separated brethren, and scholars can give of His history, with the truth proper to particular points of view, such as the cultural and the sociological.

Granted that fidelity to the Tradition of the Church has been assured, there remains for the teacher to discover the best ways to reach the minds of youth by briefly reviewing psycho-sociological principles applicable to adolescents and by establishing guidelines for presenting salvation history to adolescents.

2. Psycho-Sociological Principles

A. Psychological Dominant

The preadolescent, torn as he is between childhood and adolescence, is essentially capricious. At this age, the young person vacillates from one to the other, depending upon the circumstances. He finds himself in a virtual no-man's-land, neither one nor the other. Moreover, he is passing from the objective interests of childhood to the subjective imaginations and dreams that characterize adolescence. What is difficult is that in a class there will frequently be mingling of preadolescents still turned towards childhood and others tending towards adolescence, a heterogeneous group in age and mentality.

GROUP I	GROUP II
Preadolescents turned towards childhood	*Preadolescents tending towards adolescence*
Hyperactivity — sociability — gang spirit — group action — taste for practical accomplishments, for the definite and the objective.	Imaginative and heroic ardor — interest in heroes, sports and movie stars — sentimental fervor — fascination for sentimental situations —egocentric bent to self-analysis— dreaminess.

B. Consequences of This Psychological Dominant

a. When the class is heterogeneous as to age and mentality, what is the teacher to do?

Adapt instruction to the greater number, and widely vary methodology in plans and themes.

Observe the evolution of the class throughout the year. In general, as the year progresses and spring comes, the students in Group I rapidly move towards Group II.

b. When the majority of the class belong to Group I, what is the teacher to do?

He can follow a program which deals with the historical, a program which is clear and well-defined. He need not hesitate to insist on memorization and perfection in practical activities. He may alternate between methodological directives 1 and 2 (discussed in sections which are to follow) without in any way neglecting the very objective elements of learning and culture. The themes will insist more on the *value* of action, on the value of a *model* to be followed for the attainment of a given end, rather than on the values of interpersonal relations and self-discovery.

c. When the majority of the class belong to Group II, what is to be done?

Insist on methodological rule (procedure described subsequently under 3 and 5), and choose preference themes which favor self-analysis and the discovery of ideal values.

C. The Law of the Milieu

a. Many preadolescents and adolescents are enmeshed in the harsh realities of their milieu. Such a situation occurs in a working class environment and, in a general manner, wherever young people are not protected by a strong social structure, such as that of the Christian family and school. Young boys and girls at grips with the world are soon forced into a realistic and social way of acting; they must find their place, they must live, they must have a good job. They quickly pass from personal to objective interests. The preadolescent and the adolescent phases, periods of self-awareness, seem to be skipped. These phases are accelerated for those who take courses that do not prepare for college. On the other hand, adolescence in many respects seems to be prolonged for those who go on to college.

b. Consequences of the law of the milieu. To the extent that preadolescents are protected and their childhood is prolonged (the objective period), they will love concrete facts (battles and heroes), and geographical, historical realities concerning biblical personages if the latter are made to live for them.

On the contrary, full-fledged peradolescents will very quickly seek to discover themselves and to assert themselves among people, thus achieving socialization. They are less interested in Abraham than in modern saints, Christians of today, struggling with the same problems as theirs. Consequently, Abraham cannot be presented to preadolescents merely as an interesting historical figure. He must be of vital importance to the preadolescent's life situation here and now.

Finally, preadolescents will be less inclined to subjective analysis, to introspection. They will be less inclined to look at themselves and to evaluate themselves through religious reflections. They seek rather to act with forethought and to lay a religious foundation upon which to build their lives. Less interested in the deep meaning of things, they seek, above all, guidance in religion.

Let special stress be laid on the different reactions of boys and girls to biblical personages. Confronted with heroes, boys and girls react differently, and what is essentially different is the mode of relationship. It is sometimes said that boys are interested in the exterior drama of the personage, in his deeds of valor and war, and girls in the interior, psychological drama. Such analysis does not seem too accurate. It seems rather than boys and girls are equally interested in the interior drama expressed in an exterior setting.

However, boys and girls are not interested in the same interior drama, nor even in the same exterior setting. Thus, girls like the prophet Osee because he had trouble with his wife. When girls study the story of Moses, they ask, "What became of Moses' sister?" This is not a boy's question. Boys are fascinated by the story of the Egyptians chasing the Hebrews during the Exodus, and they ask questions about the plagues of Egypt and the techniques of the tricks performed by Pharao's magicians.

Boys look for that which excites and flatters the manly personality. Focusing on the aspect of power, they thrill to a dramatic action which appeals to their self-assertiveness. Hence their taste for the absolute, for combat, for gripping with moral problems, for success in action. Hence also their search for dynamic leadership.

Girls seek what may give value to their lives in relation with others. What counts with them is the sentimental or affective dimension. This relational, sentimental, or affective life is as strong in boys as in girls, but it has a different object in each. Boys seek the ideal virile personality; girls, a feminine ideal.

Boys become absorbed in the personality of the hero and find in it strength, an ideal, along with enlightenment in their search for personal identity.

Girls identify with persons in the relatedness to others, with the attitudes of heroes or personages in their relationship to another; and girls do so in order to acquire better knowledge of themselves, together with moral support and strength.

c. Hero worship in the various stages of adolescence. When studying the catechesis of salvation history for adolescents, it is highly useful and profitable to consider the role of hero worship in the development of the students. The teacher discovers how the adolescent matures to young manhood and young womanhood largely as a result of the fundamental process of identification with heroes.

PREADOLESCENTS. "First of all, in the hero, I discover myself, I measure myself, I gauge myself both as *different* and *talented*. I experience myself in reverie and in action. Not only do I dream of Tarzan, Batman, or 007, but I go *with my pals* on a search for underground caverns. *I experience a certain capability within myself.*"

"I discover and measure the tonus and the value of my religious attitudes with respect to God and the saints. Not only do I find myself in the hero, but I fortify myself still more in my dreams about him; I grow up under his influence, and I goad myself on to the best."

Preadolescene is the time when one greatly idealizes personages. It is the age when one is most disillusioned by the discovery that idealized teachers still remain men. It is the age when maladjusted children refuse to admit the poverty of their parents: "In my home, everything is beautiful." But even when faced with a sublime hero, the preadolescent becomes very little involved; essentially, he is a dreamer. His level of autonomy is yet too weak for action, involvement, or choice. His age is not one of action, but one of building up of values in view of an invisible structure destined to appear much later.

ADOLESCENTS. Adolescents want to study personages "that are worth our while." For example, they say of Father Charles de Foucauld: "Yes, but we want to see him in his struggles; we want to be told about his life before his conversion. Too much is said about his life after conversion without our knowing how he arrived at that stage." Here, the change is characteristic: adolescents seek heroic personages not so much to know themselves as to find out what to do. They seek the hero to fortify themselves and to gain security by identifying with him.

"Why do you like the hero?" the catechist may ask. Adolescents reply: "Because he shows me what I should do."—"Because heroes give us courage and show us how to act."—"Because the hero restores my faith."

Often the notion of sanctity, of personal holiness, is presented to the adolescent in such a way that it soon seems to be clear that holiness is completely out of his reach. There is nothing that an adolescent appreciates more than competence. If the saints were presented as the truly human men and women they were, the adolescents would be able to realize that sanctity is certainly within their grasp.

In preadolescence, the hero fascinates as a statue might fascinate; in adolescence, the hero acquires the value guide with all that the word may denote and connote of attractiveness and heroism. Idealism diminishes; realism grows. Adolescents pass little by little from dreams to timid attempts at action.

OLDER ADOLESCENTS. The taste for long-ago-and-faraway romantic heroes dies out with the beginnings of adolescence. As one approaches young manhood, the heroic characters are loved because they help the older adolescent to become involved in the world. "The person who is a success ushers me into the adult world." The condition of acceptance is that the person must be a "realistic model," someone who is highly regarded, who has known success, and on whom one may truly count. They identify themselves with the "star" of their group even to the point of adopting his manner of speaking, of walking, of kneeling. Imitation speaks very eloquently of the search for social involvement. Certainly all studies seem to show that Pope John XXIII and President John F. Kennedy captured the imagination of many young people and provided them with the incentive to give of themselves for the good of humanity. The adult is no longer a hero-worshiper; he is led by the Spirit; he lives in a world of persons to whom he gives himself and from whom he receives. But in the darker hours of life, is he not likely to return to some of his former ideals?

In summary, the line of evolution of hero worship in the various stages of adolescence seems to be drawn from idealization to realism, from dreams to reality, from search for self to search for social commitment.

3. **Three Methods.** In keeping with the tradition of the Church and with modern psychology. three major methods of approach are presented. Then a number of procedures aimed at implementing these methods are outlined. The first two methods apply especially to preadolescents in Group II. (See 2 A above.) The catechist passes from one method to the next according to the needs of the moment.

A. Catechesis Through Identification with Biblical Personages in Their Relation to God

DEFINITION. Following this method, the student identifies with a biblical personage and is called upon to experience here and now that person's openness to the Word of God illuminating his intelligence and transforming his life.

PSYCHOLOGICAL FOUNDATION. Identification is a psychological mechanism by which the student *more or less consciously* fashions his conduct and his character by modeling himself on another person. A value is thus discovered through this person by *participation* in his being and in his relationships.

Identification occurs each time a developing personality seeks (always more or less consciously) to discover in aonther person the ideal type according to which he will mold his own personality. The relationship thus created consists in a phenomenon of osmosis by which the life of another becomes one's own and by which one discovers one's life in that of another. Psychology insists strongly on the part identification plays during the time of adolescence.

PRINCIPLES AND PROCEDURE

1. Give primacy to the Word of God. In catechesis it is of capital importance to give *primacy to the Word of God* rather than to the attitude of men. Take, for example, the catechesis of the bibiical account of Moses and the burning bush. It must be made clear that the attitude of Moses is transformed not by reason of a good, natural, moral influence upon him, but because God grapples with him and *reveals* something to him. It can never be overemphasized sufficiently how most of the difficulties in salvation history catechesis stem from the fact that teachers stress too strongly the human aspect and not primarily that of God, who reveals the kingdom and thus transforms man.

2. Achieve identification on the pedagogical plane.

a. The starting point demands the catechist's personal convictions.

In order that one person may identify with another person, there must be some *real* connection between them. The person with whom one identifies must represent in some way a value for the other. Psychologists point out the adolescent has a multiplicity of needs—psychological, social, physical, spiritual—which must be satisfied. A thing acquires value when it is perceived as capable of fulfilling a need. In catechesis, therefore, biblical personages must be seen as having a universal relevance and, at the same time, a certain value with regard to the group. Now, it is certain that *in themselves* biblical personages are representative of man. Abraham, Moses, David, and especially Jesus Christ are all men who have been profoundly affected by the Word of God. They stand at the point of the most intense communion between the human creature and God who calls. It is certain, too, that biblical personages are *values*, not indeed because of the natural heroism which they may manifest, but because of the marvelous transformation of their lives which resulted from their receptivity to the Word of God.[1]

b. How does the catechesis proceed from the starting point? How do we manage pedagogically to have the biblical personage being studied perceived as a value and as representative of man? Essentially, it is through the mediation of the catechist, inasmuch as the catechist here and now reflects the living Church, that the biblical personage will appear as "value" and as "representative." The important factor is *the quality of the relationship between the catechist and the young*. The catechist must, as he is the witness of the Church, be for the young a place of encounter between the past biblical fact and their own personal situation. To the extent that the catechist appears to be united *both* to the young *and* to the Word of God historicized in Abraham, to that extent will the young best encounter God speaking to them. It can be said that in the catechist Abraham lives on, and because

---

1 Schema

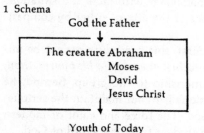

God the Father

The creature Abraham
Moses
David
Jesus Christ

Youth of Today

1. Representative of man.

2. Value: inasmuch as it leads to a new way of life already transformed by the reality of the Promised Land.

the catechist is linked up with the young, all are involved when God calls Abraham. (Abraham — Catechist — Church — Youth of Today). The catechist must truly love his students. The students readily sense and respond to the catechist's attitude.

c. The procedure should be considered further. The catechist, as noted above, is the "vital mediator" through whom identification between the group and the biblical personage is achieved. That is the essential point. Besides the way of being, however, there is a way of speaking which facilitates identification. In other words, how may the child identify with the biblical personage through the words of the catechist?

Essentially, the catechist must present the past event with constant *allusions* and *references* to the youth whom he is addressing. This procedure can produce remarkable effects. When the catechist includes individuals in his presentation in a charitable and understanding manner, the class responds very spontaneously. However, this procedure requires practised skill and tact. What he says should thus seem stamped with the historical validity of the personage (customs of Abraham) and with the actual representation which the young tend to make for themselves, caught up as they are today in the journey towards the Promised Land.

There is an associative procedure by which we link the actual deed with the past event, thanks to images, deeds, symbols, and words which resound profoundly in the actual world situation of the group and at the same time may characterize the past biblical event.

Often simple words suffice to build a bridge between the biblical figure and actual life. Often, too, the catechist may associate the historical presentation of the personage with facts and situations relevant to the actual experience of the group, either by comparison or by symbolic association.

Two remarks are in order. First, this procedure cannot be imposed from the outside; *each catechist must devise his own method*, depending on his type of relationship to the group. Second, he must not fall into cheap sensationalism, but maintain the seriousness proper to the Word of God. The force and color of modern allusions must not distract the student from the Word of God.

The relevance of the Word of God to the world situation today can be effectively brought home to the students through photographs of current events and conditions. Often a quotation from Holy Scripture used as a caption for a photograph can have remarkable impact. *Newsweek* magazine recently provide a striking example of this procedural technique. A photograph portraying a weeping Vietnamese mother clutching her dying child was described as a modern Pieta. Scriptural quotations, like "And God saw that it was good," or "Lord, when did we see You hungry?" can be made relevant to our own times throught skillful use of photographs.

B. Retrospection as a Method of Catechesis

Retrospection is a method by which the catechist makes the group relive an enactment and an interpretation of past events using some key idea as the core of the interpretation. The catechist appeals to the imagination of the students and tries to recreate the scene with all its inherent implications. The topic of catechesis may be making personal contact with Christ in the liturgy. Two young men who have "had a lot of religious instruction" are bored. Their faith is dull. "We had this over and over," they say. Jesus sharpens their faith on the way to Emmaus. Using a story technique, He shows them that all written in the Scripture refers to Him. Their hearts are on fire as they hear the word of God. "Faith comes by hearing," says St. Paul. But the nourishment of their faith is not yet complete. They come to recognize the food in the breaking of the bread. Twice at Mass Christians are in personal touch with Christ in the way He establishes contact: in the Liturgy of the Word and in the Liturgy of the Eucharist. (See Luke 24:24ff.)

VALUE. It is hardly necessary to discuss the value of this retrospective procedure. It is the most directly catechetical, since it give a proper religious interpretation of history. It is the "Memoria" in act. Moreover, the point of view through which the interpretation is made is generally a personage at a crucial moment of his life. The method has double value in that the young identify with the personage himself.

A related procedure is to have the students write accounts of biblical events in their own words. An interesting project is to have students write up incidents which may have taken place during the hidden years of Christ's life. Specific titles can be suggested, such as, "The Disagreement," "His Favorite Friends," "The Fishing Trip." Usually such essays are very revealing and intimate. This is *not* catechesis, but it helps the students to identify.

C. Use of Analogous Situation in Catechesis

DEFINITION. This method consists in setting out from the presentation of a current event or group situation in order to transform it in the light of a biblical situation analogous to it. For example, is God relevant to the young man who wants to succeed in life? Is God relevant to movie stars? Can one live a Christian life in New York? Such examples dramatize the problem of the pagan world confronted with the Christian ideal. Analogous biblical situations are that of Elias in the desert and of John the Baptist protesting what he finds in the godless world about him. Other analogies are to be found in the life of St. Anthony in the desert and in the Christian during the liturgical season of Lent. The establishment of the State of Israel after World War II by the Jews is strikingly analogous to the biblical Exodus.

VALUE. Pedagogically, this method has value especially to adolescents because of the *interest of the adolescent in himself, in life, in current events*. It is valuable also in that it constitutes *a call to action,* to the transformation of the heart and to conversion.

LIMITS. Note that it is difficult with this type of catechetical presentation to develop a structure of systematic and coordinated thought. The method stems from intuition rather than reason; it elicits certain attitudes towards events rather than systematic planning of one's life. Excessive use of this method can lead to restlessness and disorientation. Finally, this method makes difficult the implementation of a systematic program. Therefore, in places where a systematic catechesis is given, the catechist will use the three methods, depending on which biblical figure or fact is being taught, thus indicating clearly that it is the program which has priority in catechesis.

4. Procedures and Directives for Presenting Biblical Personages. How does the catechist present personages from sacred history? The rules which follow are suggested as aids in presenting

the biblical message in a way palatable to preadolescents. It is assumed, of course, that the catechist knows when and how to vary the method of presentation.

1. *Start with a typical event which is colorful and capable of stimulating interest.* For example, present Elias, arms folded, standing before the priests of Baal, who are shouting to the heavens for the altar of sacrifice to be consumed. Elias thinks out loud and expresses *his interpretation.* A scene, chosen for its dramatic value, may be taken anywhere in the life of the personage. The presentation need not always begin with birth or vocation. Shun any pattern of presentation that would lead to monotony.

2. *Stress the important events in the life of the personage.* The catechist cannot tell everything about the life of a biblical personage. He must look for the moments of highest interest, moments when his dialogue with God involved him the most profoundly, moments when he committed himself fully. One or two key occasions, one or two highlights of his life will help adolescents to penetrate into the interior drama of the personage. Moses' story, for example, might center around the incidents of the burning bush, Mount Sinai, and the golden calf.

3. *Sketch the biblical personage with realism.* If the catechist wishes adolescents to identify with a hero, he must introduce them to a very concrete person in a concrete *historical* situation. What is meaningful is not his situation in scientific, general history, but the *details of his epoch.* Try to *delineate* the personage, highlighting his emotions and his difficulties. Whatever the teacher can find to say regarding his physical stature, when that is possible, his clothing, and his gestures, will incarnate the personage and make him live. For example, Amos was a shepherd. Speak about the customs of shepherds. Recourse to details provided by archeology is often of great assistance in giving realistic portrayals.

4. *Present the event in epic style; make use of contrasts.* Adolescents like the epic style. The presentation of a personage should take this into account. Conflict and contrast among personages and their situations make them better understood and appreciated. The contrast between the idolatry of the people of God and the unshakable fidelity of Moses to God, the serenity of Isaia in con-

trast to the restlessness of Achaz, the fire of an Amos and the gentleness of Osee, and the difference of opinion between Peter and Paul at the council of Jerusalem exemplify the contrasts in which the Bible abounds.

5. *Have the details of the story converge on a theme or a spiritual attitude.* It is most important that catechetical discussion be faithful to the interior unity of a theme. It is the theme which must be interiorized and integrated into the life of the student. The adolescent will perceive the meaning of the details if they cluster around one theme. He will remember them. Let the theme be true to the biblical message and, at the same time, adapted to the adolescent. For example, the drama of *repentance* in the sin of David as well as the heroism of his life and the courage to admit his wrong could be a unifying theme.[2]

6. *Let the presentation invite the adolescent himself to relive the spiritual encounter of the biblical personage.* For example, the encounter between Moses and God must place the adolescent himself face to face with God. *The teacher must endeavor to foster an attitude of prayer, of spiritual religious reflection, of meditation.* By means of an analogy, a reading, a more serious attitude at times, the teacher must try to initiate the mysterious spiritual encounter in which the adolescent becomes aware of God and commits his life to Him.

7. *Vary the manner of presentation.* In general, the catechist gives lessons aiming at a gradual education in the faith. At certain times, he gives talks, especially prepared and thought over during prayer, aiming at an evangelization, at a profound conversion. Such lessons constitute summits in our teaching. For example, of three lessons on Moses, the catechist foresees a climax lesson on Moses' encounter with God on Mount Sinai. Perhaps the first two lessons might involve the active participation of the students in a discussion or project. A final commentary by the catechist will effectively

---

2 It may be difficult to present to adolescents themes which are, in spite of their difficulty, objectively important, such as the Covenant, the Law. To be faithful to the message, one must mention them, without necessarily focusing an entire lesson on these themes. Once again, however, background details associated with such subjects will arouse and sustain adequate interest.

allow the students to realize the significance of what they have experienced or discovered. Finally, the catechist must foresee lessons which will be *more didactic*, aiming more at intellectual formation.

5. **Presentation of the Miraculous in the Bible.** Stressing the marvelous or miraculous in the Bible, for example, the walls of waves which rose on both sides of the Hebrews as they crossed the Red Sea, constitutes a literary genre. At a certain time and in a certain context, this procedure spontaneously evoked spiritual meanings. Thus, the walls of water evoked the extraordinary power of Yahweh, who saves His people "with a strong hand and an outstretched arm."

However, out of context, this literary device, instead of revealing spiritual significations, may become a stumbling block. A boy who asks his teacher, "How high did the waves in the Red Sea rise?" shows that the marvelous, instead of being a vehicle for spiritual realities, turned his mind away towards material realities.

What must the catechist do so that biblical marvels may fulfill their purpose? At first glance, the epic style seems awkward and primitive, unmanageable for teachers of objective and rational mentality. Perhaps one must be something of a poet to be able to deal with biblical marvels according to the truth of their meaning. The biblical marvel cannot be fathomed unless the student is familiar with the concept of literary form. He must be shown the many figurative forms which he himself uses every day, for example, "He broke his heart." The teacher who finds himself hampered by the epic style may avoid it as much as possible. To others, a more effective approach might be the method of retrospection and of association in order to give primary importance to spiritual meanings and thus to avoid the dangers of reducing everything to a natural explanation. Thus, presenting the waves of the Red Sea through Miriam's intepretation of them gives them their real dimensions, and the student will be led to understand that Miriam's quite oriental exaltation is caused, not by the waves, but by the power of Yahweh.

In the presentation of biblical events, three pitfalls are to be avoided.

a. *To present as historical an event which is not so, or at least whose historical validity is seriously questioned* because of the literary genre involved. Men have become skeptics with regard to the Bible because they discovered at the end of their studies that facts which had been presented to them as historical were not so. Catechists today must face this very delicate problem. Many events of the Old Testament are presented in grade school as historical occurrences, and the high school catechist is faced with the task of resolving the ardent crises in the indignant adolescent who feels that he was misled.

b. *To present real events, especially important ones, without sufficient historical consistency.* Some teachers give a catechesis so spiritual, so linked with symbolism that is lacks rigor and solidity, and risks leading souls either to a more or less sentimental acceptance, or later, to skepticism or denial of faith.

c. *To make an awkward presentation of facts whose historicity is contested.* A catechist who presents biblical events in such a way that they elicit critical reflection outside the pale of faith would be unfaithful to the intentions of the Church and the sacred writers. The scriptural records aim at awakening not criticism or doubt, but faith.

In order to avoid these pitfalls, here are some guidelines:

a. *Study the material to be taught.* The background provided by a textbook for the child is never enough for the teacher.

b. *Establish historical facts* with a maximum of realism and concrete details in order to anchor them in history and geography. Make use of atlases, slides, books, and other aids. Allude to the student's social studies program. Resort to the scientific disciplines of anthropology, archeology, and philosophy that have made a significant contribution to the advancement of biblical research.

c. *Present the essential facts* (for example, the events of Easter) with some support from apologetics, thus giving security to the intelligence. Apologetics should depend not on historical details which might be questioned (for example, the chronology of apparitions), but on a synthetic view of the problems at issue, (for example, the *fact* of the apparitions). The catechist should not neglect the support of a number of arguments from classical apologetics, yet some rational approach seems more and more important in the school context of the young of today, a context which distinguishes carefully between facts and interpetation, and which tends to equate the Bible with the interpretations of an ethnic group.

d. *As to the facts and details introduced into the Gospel for theological reasons* or because of the need for historical or symbolical coherence, *the catechist might play down their historicity*, by stressing strongly their meaning. For example, he ought not to insist on the historicity of the forty days before Ascension, but on its significance for the Church: the Exodus took forty years before man came from death to new life; the number forty is a parallel as Jesus prepares for His final visible Exodus to the Father and the consequent descent of His Spirit that all may live the new life of the redeemed Son of God

Or *the catechist might present certain events from the Church's point of view*. For example, with an effort to emulate the perfection of the primitive communities, the early Church interpreted these events and insisted on their meaning. Thus, in order to avoid certain obscurities concerning the episode of the Magi, the teacher might tell it using a first-century mosaic which depicts Mary presenting Jesus to the Magi, *symbol of all the nations*. He will insist particularly not on the precise nationality of the Magi, but on the affirmation of the Church, according to which the Son of God came not only for the Jews, but for the whole universe and particularly the pagans who searched in vain for signs. This method is perfectly true to the catechesis of the Church such as she expresses it in her liturgy.

e. *Textual criticism must be avoided* with adolescents whose mentality is immature. Still less may the teacher demolish, with a superior smile, details which the young esteem as historical. Incapable of understanding such a procedure, the children conclude: "We no longer know what is true and what is false in the Bible."

With adolescents, the catechist must always be positive, not destructive. He must speak in such a way that his catechesis will include, not the details of modern exegesis, but its spirit, its fundamental theory, which aims at stressing the meaning and the solidity of the biblical events.

6. How to Study a Biblical Text. Caution against emphasizing textual criticism of the Bible in catechesis of adolescents should not preclude the necessity for profound study of the biblical text in the catechist's preparation. On the contrary, from time to time, it is necessary to analyze a sentence or a word. Such analysis is often used in Protestant Sunday School classes, and its advantage is considerable. It familiarizes the young Christian with the text of the Bible and consequently permits him to read it intelligently and profitably.

a. *Speak rather of meaning than of literary genre.* Adolescents are little inclined to the historical sense and to the relativity of literary genres. There is no question about the value of *general* discussion of literary genres. But it is important to give the *general signification* of a passage of the Bible by studying a biblical figure and situating it in the context of the whole work. For example, set the temptation of Jesus in the messianic context.

b. *Define the words.* It is necessary to define with precision the important words of the Bible to correct any false meaning which they might take on from modern usage. It is necessary to penetrate the true meaning of words contained in ancient texts. This is doubtless valuable when there is a question of explaining "Adam's rib," but even more so when key words are at stake such as kingdom, miracle, demons, hell, flesh, spirit. Most of these words might be used without the students' really knowing what they mean.

The Bible remains a closed book for many, mainly because the old meanings of many words have become obsolete. The teacher should stress *before all else,* for memorization purposes, the meaning of the words. This is the one occasion when he has the opportunity to spark genuine student interest in the Bible.

Index